JOURNEY TO UNDERSTANDING

Joy of a Commissioned Pastor

By
Michael V. Slayter, D.V.M.

Copy Rights

All Rights Reserved

All rights reserved. No part of this publication may be reproduced, distributed, or transmitted in any form or by any means, including photocopying, recording, or other electronic or mechanical methods, without the prior written permission of the publisher, except in the case of brief quotations embodied in critical reviews and certain other non-commercial uses permitted by copyright law.

This book is dedicated to my wife, Jane, who is my compass and my anchor – the most selfless person I have ever known before and throughout the fifty plus years we have been together.

"There were times when I felt that something better and truer than my words was speaking through my words. There were times when I felt they were only words. There were times when the words seem to fall dead from my lips and other times when I could see only too clearly how effective they were being. And maybe I entirely misjudged which time was which. I don't know. I know only that Barth is surely right when he says that no one risks the wrath of God more perilously than the minister in the pulpit, and yet at the same time I know that, as a minister, there are few places I would rather be. The excitement and challenge of it. The chance that something better than what you are can happen, that something more than you know can be spoken and heard."

Frederick Buechner in: *Now and Then*

Acknowledgments:

In chronological order, my first acknowledgment and words of sincere thanks go to the late Reverend M. Richard Underwood, my pastor in Whitinsville, MA, who allowed me to step up to the podium and deliver my first sermon. His congenial personality invited me to ask dumb questions and get ten times the answer I had bargained for. I never felt looked down upon in his presence.

Austin Reichert, my dear friend from Whitinsville, Massachusetts, who was and is a talented speaker and ordained ruling elder in PC(USA). Along with Pastor Underwood, he gave me encouragement and positive feedback that fueled my efforts as a rookie.

Dr. Frank Allen, former pastor of First Presbyterian Church of Kissimmee, Florida, guided me as I immersed myself in the didactics of The Dubuque University Theological Seminary. Frank never spoon-fed answers to me, rather answered my questions with questions. Frank taught me how to think like a preacher.

Rev. Harold Thornton, former Parish Associate of First Presbyterian Church of Kissimmee, spent many hours with me discussing scripture and preaching techniques. His support added immeasurably to my growing confidence in many ways, and I appreciate his willingness to write the foreword for this book.

Dr. Timothy Slemmons, professor at The University of Dubuque Theological Seminary, brought out the best in us as he taught my introductory course in preaching. We have stayed in touch over the years, and he graciously agreed to be the editor of this book. He was perfect for this job, in my opinion, because I knew he suffered no fools, which is exactly what I needed to finish this project.

Rev. Adam Bowling is Pastor of First United Presbyterian Church of Dale City, Virginia (my current home church). Since I left Central Florida Presbytery and entered National Capital Presbytery, the entire commissioning process had to be repeated, apart from the seminary courses I had taken. Adam stayed with me throughout the entire process with tenacious encouragement and support. His confidence in my role in this new church home added to my resolve to finish what I had started. I now serve God's purpose as Parish Assistant under Adam's guidance as Senior Pastor.

Table of Contents

Foreword i

Prologue iii

Chapter One: Holy Dilemma 1

Chapter Two: May I Ask Who's Calling? 13

Chapter Three: God's Mailbox 26

Chapter Four: Faith or Belief or Imagination 40

Chapter Five: Ambassadors of the Kingdom 51

Chapter Six: To Love is To Live 62

Chapter Seven: You Only Live Twice 73

Chapter Eight: Shepherds 83

Chapter Nine: By Their Fruits 97

Chapter Ten: Smell The Coffee 108

Chapter Eleven: Debts? What Debts? 120

Chapter Twelve: Never-ending tale 131

Foreword

I met Mike Slayter at church. We talked after the service and walked together out to the parking lot. I noticed he was driving a Mazda Miata, which is little Japanese two-seater very much like the MGB I had owned once. I asked him a set up question: "Have you seen the Miata trunk?" Mike looked puzzled and then I dropped the punch line to my joke: "Oh don't worry, nobody else has seen one either." We both laughed and thus began the relationship of easy laughter and conversation about experiences we shared.

I was in the early days of retirement, having finished 35 years as a pastor in the PCUSA. Mike was about to be a retired pathologist in veterinary medicine. I was the parish associate in the First Presbyterian Church in Kissimmee, Florida and he was still working reading animal biopsies at home, but not for long. A year later, he was also retired and ready to take on new challenges.

Over time, I observed Mike was doing a great job recruiting and training lay folk for Stephen Ministry in the church. He had a vision for equipping members to be trained and useful listeners in the lives of members who needed someone to just care about them.

It really didn't surprise me when he told me he was preparing for the ministry of a Commissioned Pastor. The training would involve completing seminary courses in pastoral ministry and I had confidence that he would use his preparation to be very helpful and encouraging to the members of churches in transition.

Mike's book is about the journey of serving and learning as a Commissioned Pastor. He distills his experience around topics that are real in ministry. He does it with an accessible style that will resonate with fellow pastors who come to their Commissioned Pastor calling from many different life experiences. His book could be for personal encouragement, or the chapters could be a discussion starter for a Commissioned Pastor support group. It's all about the journey of ministry so join with Mike as you travel the ways of useful ministry.

-Harold Thornton, M.Div.
Kissimmee, Florida

Prologue

Since I was ten years old, I can remember wanting to be a veterinarian. I don't know what started it, except maybe it was when I sat and listened to Uncle Jake, my maternal grandmother's half-brother, tell of his life's work. Uncle Jake graduated as J. C. Frazier, DVM, from University of Georgia, School of Veterinary Medicine, in the early 50's. By the time I was old enough to understand part of what he was describing as a typical day at work, he had settled in Greenville, South Carolina and had a thriving mixed animal practice. I could sit and listen for hours to his tales of challenges and rewards that today sound like chapters out of *All Creatures Great and Small*.

I was certain that private practice was my destiny when I graduated with my own DVM degree from Texas A&M in 1969, but the conflict in Viet Nam had changed everyone's life. I knew the draft board would catch up with me eventually, so I preemptively decided to take an Air Force commission and follow the footsteps of my father, who was a retired Air Force officer. My plan, however, was to serve my two years in uniform and then go back to my original dream of private practice, which is what I did. But there was something missing that left me searching for the gratification I needed. In school, I did well in the clinical classes where we worked with live animals belonging to live human owners, but I had acquired a real affinity for the esoteric, the minutia, the hidden details of basic sciences that clinical practitioners simply didn't have time to dwell on. For example, a clinician may have a thorough understanding of what pneumonia is and all the various causes of it, but pondering and meditating on the aspects of all the microscopic changes and chemical mediators of inflammation in lung tissue were details outside of the routine clinical approach.

I ended up returning to military service where I had a chance to receive further training in a specialty that would challenge me and capture my interest. I decided that pathology held the answers and the satisfaction I was looking for and, after a few failed attempts, I found myself in a training program that would equip me to be involved in some very in-depth research and later would qualify me to be a major player in diagnostic work after I retired from the military. In 1987, I achieved board-certification in veterinary pathology.

Looking back, it sounds like I was very focused on my career, but in the background, my Christian foundations were always with me. I had grown up in a church environment of the 50's and 60's that did not encourage much out-of-the-box thinking. There were rules about morality that one did not challenge even if they sounded like Puritan restrictions from the seventeenth century. No alcohol, no dancing, no mixed-gender swimming, and Rock n Roll music was the work of the devil. During a year when my dad was stationed overseas by himself, my mother, my sister, and I lived near our grandparents' home. Each year, a guest minister would be invited to their church to preach every night for a week. Every night, he brought us fiery sermons. I saw teenagers in tears for fear of hellfire and damnation.

I saw adults, baptized believers, come forward to ask for a re-baptizing in case the first one didn't work. It reminded me of getting a booster shot for tetanus. What put me over the edge in later years was hearing that my wife's baptism in the Roman Catholic Church was not recognized by the denomination to which I belonged. Around 1979, while stationed at Chanute Air Force Base, I found a small Presbyterian church in Rantoul, Illinois that really woke up my Christian radar. The members there actually encouraged one another to push the envelope and expand their spiritual horizons. I found out later that this was not something unique to this congregation alone. There was full recognition of my wife's baptism. Now I had two realms of thought to keep me busy, pathology and the Presbyterian Church, both of which could be viewed as different portals to what I needed to know. The church helped me understand the enormity of God's grace and the microscope showed me the intricacy of God's creation.

I was first ordained as a deacon, then as an elder in the early 80's at Frederick Presbyterian Church, Frederick, Maryland while I was stationed at Fort Detrick.

After I retired from the military, I found myself working as a pathologist for IDEXX laboratories and living in Northbridge, Massachusetts. I attended a Presbyterian church there in which the pastor, Rick Underwood, would occasionally ask a particular elder named Austin Reichert to fill the pulpit in the pastor's absence. Austin had fine-tuned, remarkable Bible knowledge and was a good speaker. He had a sense of organization and knew how to connect the dots with a gospel message. My wife, Jane, had been watching my Christian growth journey over the years and asked me why I had not volunteered to fill the pulpit as well. I think I said something about not wanting to infringe on Austin's domain, but Jane saw through that deception and knew my excuse was really a doubt in my own ability and she dared me to try. So, I asked and, surprisingly, Rick and Austin both welcomed my offer. It suddenly dawned on me that I had just volunteered to do something I had never done before but I had no intention of backing out. With no particular date in mind, I began preparing my first sermon. It took me about a month to get it in final, polished form. I didn't even know what a lectionary was. I just picked a topic and went after it. Forgiveness seemed like a topic with meat on it, something I could get my amateurish teeth into, so that's what I hatched out. When Rick finally approached me with a date, I felt my stomach in my throat.

Public speaking had never been a problem for me. But it had always been centered around concrete scientific facts and laboratory findings. I always had pictures, charts, and data to illustrate my point. My education and the topics I lived with were always about hard facts, not belief through faith. Scientific hypotheses may be in part based on faith, but the conclusion has always been immersed in hard facts. Sermon preparation and preaching are not hard science as we know it in a traditional sense. What I did know was that if you really want to know about a certain thing, try putting together a twenty-minute monologue on the subject. In preparing my first sermon, I came to realize how much I did not know. I marveled at the fact that there were those individuals who could do this task every week, all the while paying attention to running a church and shepherding a congregation.

I don't like doing anything haphazardly or half-heartedly. Just as when I decided to go into pathology, I wanted this newly discovered challenge to take me to a higher level.

I finally retired from IDEXX Laboratories and moved to Kissimmee, Florida. Along the way, I had heard bits and pieces about lay ministers in the Presbyterian Church (USA) and some sort of validation process leading to the status of Commissioned Ruling Elder (now known as Commissioned Pastor). I asked my pastor, Dr. Frank Allen, about this and he directed me to the correct page in the Book of Order that addressed the details and process. Years before, after I had achieved my certification in pathology, I had promised myself I would never go back to school in any sense, nor would I let myself be subjected to any more scrutiny and judgement by some committee. Needless to say, I broke that promise and enrolled in online courses at University of Dubuque Theological Seminary, with the approval of the Session of Elders from my church.

I was commissioned on December 6, 2016, in Central Florida Presbytery. In 2018, I attended the first week of Transitional Ministry training at Montreat, NC, simply as a matter of continuing education. As luck (God's providence?) would have it, my last hurrah in Florida was to serve as interim pastor of my home church, First Presbyterian Church of Kissimmee, for ten months. We moved to Northern Virginia to be near our oldest son, and I applied for the same status in the National Capital Presbytery. After jumping through many hoops, I reached that goal on January 24, 2023. Many thanks to Pastor Adam Bowling of First United Presbyterian Church of Dale City, Virginia, for guiding me through that rigorous process.

I have come to a point in my life where I have accumulated enough training, experience, mistakes, anecdotes, and thoughts that I feel the compulsion to share it with others. My purpose in this book is to illustrate concepts and ideas of which I had only a vague grasp or a partial comprehension as well as some I have probably used ineffectively until I took on the task of becoming a Commissioned Pastor. My hope is that by describing my own learning curve I can encourage others to consider a path, any path, of leading others along the Christian journey as a dedicated disciple, Commissioned Pastor or not, and to follow the ministry of your choice with the right training and tools. My secondary purpose is directed toward anyone who has reached and passed retirement age. Don't think of yourself as beyond the ability to learn something new. You still have years ahead of you. I am seventy-seven as I write this. You can be as productive as your imagination allows.

At age seventy, I threw myself into the deep end of the pool and started my attempt to make sense of what I really believed. One can only tread water for so long before a decision must be made as to which direction to swim. Funny how you come to grips with yourself when you put your thoughts on paper and then ask yourself if that is really what you mean. Learning in a classroom environment is one thing, experiencing it first-hand is quite different. If you preach, let your sermons reflect that. If a sermon is meant to carry a strong message, put your heart into it. Say what you feel, what you know, not just what the book says.

I do not consider myself a bulwark of information and knowledge. But I do like to read. We learn from things we read and hear and witness, and it would be impossible to cite every source from which I have learned something of the Christian faith. My sermons come, in varying proportions, from my own thoughts and my reading from authors I tend to gravitate toward. The authors I value and have depended on most often in these chapters are Frederick Buechner, Philip Yancey, William Barclay (specifically, his Bible commentaries), Shirley Guthrie, and Henri Nouwen. There are most likely others from whom I have gleaned ideas and paraphrased, but long since forgotten where the ideas came from.

We all have a search in our hearts, whether we admit it or not. My search was for a vocabulary to say what the spirit has led me to believe.

I encourage all who write sermons to follow the idea that scripture interprets scripture (as though you did not already know that). Verses of scripture should be taken in the context of the whole Bible. Be sure to read at least a chapter preceding the chosen verses as you look for what Thomas G. Long calls the center of gravity within the pericope you have chosen as the basis of your sermon (*The Witness of Preaching*, Westminster John Knox Press, 2005). Once you have found that focus, locate a thematic reference Bible that shows how the theme of one pericope can be found in others. Then, reading the commentaries of such related passages will help you form a mental image of your sermon's theme. Above all else, put yourself into what you compose. If you're going to preach, God wants you to speak from the heart. Don't just read someone else's words. Go ahead, open your heart, bleed a little, be yourself. That's the way Jesus communicated. The best sermons are written with a sprinkle of passion and warmth. Maybe that comes from a little bit of my revival week experience as a boy. I never said it was all bad.

What follows is a series of topics I have come across in my journey up to and as a Commissioned Pastor, topics that have challenged my intellect and tickled my interests. At the end of each chapter is a haiku that I hope creates a framework around the essence of the preceding pages.

I am making myself very vulnerable with these chapters. I take constructive criticism well. But please, just walk in my shoes for a moment before you take me to the theological woodshed. I've been on a journey, and I want to tell you about it. Questions at the end of each chapter are typical of those placed at the feet of both ordained and commissioned clergy. Be ready to be blind-sided!

And, as you can imagine, now that I am retired, when my dog needs medical care, I must take her to a real veterinary clinic, stand aside and quietly watch!

Peace,
-Michael V. Slayter, DVM

Chapter One
Holy Dilemma

How often have I heard and wondered about the term, "Human Condition" and silently filed it away as something I would dive into later when I felt like it? What is the tipping point that makes unanswered questions finally have a voice that you pay attention to? I don't know, but the topic finally surfaced in my simmering kettle of a brain one day, and I set out to do some in-depth thinking and searching. I suppose there are more explanations as to its meaning than anyone could care to count. People probably use it in a variety of ways, for serving whatever message they seem to be perched on at the moment. I have my own opinion about it. I know this: it has to do with inner conflict.

Many years ago, it occurred to me that we humans carry around a trait from our prehistoric ancestors that could be called, in a pedestrian way, "selfishness." I think we all have an inner tendency to be focused on self as a carry-over from those ancient ancestors who survived from one day to the next. The animal kingdom still has this self-focus as a primary behavioral trait. I think we also still have it, but to a much more limited extent. A major part of it manifests as self-esteem. Self-esteem, next to God's grace, is our most treasured possession. It is what gets you out of bed each morning. Is that being selfish? Probably not. You decide. More about that later.

So, is this self-focused aspect of human life really diminished through some evolutionary equation? Or is it just tethered in such a way that we don't act like wild animals? It appears to me that turning our focus toward others requires a conscious process of thought, not simply a response to an instinctive urge. In most cases, one must forcibly put aside self-focusing through an intentional act or thought before one can focus on others.

That can create inner conflict. Every time we see someone in need and realize we must alter our own priorities before we can meet the needs of the other person, we feel that conflict. It is the conflict between selfless and selfish that comes in many flavors and colors, but it always reflects the same principle. And we carry it with us wherever we go.

Somewhere in the past I watched a video by someone whose name I cannot recall, but he mentioned something that doesn't require an advanced college degree to understand. He said exactly what I have been thinking all these years and that is the conflict that I have just described. He said we all have it in us, and he called it - The Human Condition!

I was just surfing through some YouTube videos, and he caught my attention. I stopped and listened for a minute and then I couldn't tear myself away. He went on to say that if we paid attention to science, specifically psychology, we would see this as a scientific epiphany. I think not. He went on to say that science can cure the problem.

That's where he lost me. I guess he did not consider the fact that countless Bible passages talk about this very thing and declare us to be in God's image, thereby having the tools to fix the problem.

God's image - I suppose we must first admit that we believe in God and, in fact, need God, before we can start talking about being in God's image. There is a nubbin of that image inside us that we carry everywhere, like DNA. But we have covered it with layers of worldly 'stuff' like onion layers. If we peel back the layers of this holy onion, layers that have names like fear, greed, pride, lust, guilt, all the things that have to do with self-focus - we find the image of God buried deep inside like a treasure covered by that conflict we call human condition.

We carry that conflict with us everywhere we go like excess baggage. In fact, we have had it for so long, we don't even know it's there.

We need God because we have layers of questions. Questions as to why we are here, what are we to do, how did we get here, where are we headed, am I okay, are you okay? Did you ever notice how many questions Jesus asked? He had more questions than statements, it seems. The average person wants simple straightforward answers that require little mental effort. At first, I thought it to be spiritual laziness, but now I think it might also be a subliminal attempt to avoid discomfort, the discomfort that comes from inner conflict, fearing that the answers to pivotal questions might leave us in a put-up-or-shut-up dilemma. As my wife often tells me, "If you can't live with the answer, don't ask the question." The dilemma posed by questions of who, what, why, where is another aspect of the human condition. Another inner conflict. And all inner conflicts are centered around God.

Those brave enough to admit it to be a bit more complicated and requiring deeper inquiry find themselves contemplating the validity and basis of two statements:
First, there is natural, general evidence of God's existence.
Second, there is specific evidence of God's existence revealed only to individuals who open their hearts and care to delve deeper into the questions and listen.

Dr. Shirley Guthrie, in his book, *Christian Doctrine*, says there is general revelation and special revelation. The first one applies to all the indirect evidence we see in nature. The synchrony of the seasons and the complexity of living things all point to a higher being and everyone can see it if they just stop and look. It starts with human initiative.

The second one applies to experience with the living God and starts with a God initiative. Think of the many covenants God made with the likes of Abraham, Moses, David, and the cup of the new covenant at the last supper. Rather than an intuitive conclusion, God makes it clear through biblical sources. Guthrie says it is not to know *something* but to know *someone*. It is to experience God's communication through the revelation of God that we receive through the Bible.

Communication is a multifactorial word we find in so many aspects of life. One simple thing about it, however, is that communication is not complete unless it is received after it is transmitted. We must first believe there is someone on the other end of the line before we pick up the phone.

British novelist, Julian Barnes, a non-believer, said, "I don't believe in God, but I miss him." In T.S. Eliot's "The Cocktail Party," Celia said, "I want to be cured of a craving for something I cannot find and the shame of not finding it.". I wonder what she was looking for. In one of his novels, Sinclair Lewis describes a conversation in which one person says to another, "On the surface, we are quite different; but deep down we are fundamentally the same. We are both desperately unhappy about something, and we don't know what it is." People who do not know God's love are unhappy - and probably don't even know it.

Speaking of novelists, most fictional writers will tell you that no story is interesting or intriguing unless there is some sort of conflict in the story line. Human nature is drawn to it like a moth to a flame.

Looking and finding: that's a challenge for anyone, even Christians. Looking and not finding: that's a point of inner conflict. I wonder how many people play mind games on themselves, entertaining imaginary images of fantasy and convince themselves it's God speaking, that they have found something? Maybe it's not a game but just a way of opening up one's thoughts and letting God step in. All too often, I find myself looking for a logical way to see God, a logical way to let God in, a logical way to understand who God is. We live in a world where logic is essential, so why should I not look for God in the same way?

My dog has her own brand of logic. It's called association. She develops certain patterns, and she associates them with a favorable outcome. She gets into and out of the car on the driver's side. She hasn't figured out how to do it on the passenger side. She has some associations that tell her what not to do because she relates it to an unfavorable outcome. My dog cannot go beyond that line of reasoning. We humans do the same thing and much more beyond that.

So, is my logic in line with God's logic? Am I so arrogant as to think I can be on His level?

Still, I cannot discount the value of human logic. Maybe we also learn by association. Much of science is based on cause and effect, which is a powerful form of association. I know of scientists who say there is no God, that science can explain everything. I ask them to tell me where the substance of the universe came from at the time of creation. I don't have an answer, but neither do they. It defies logic. But it sends a message that we need to think outside of the box. Or maybe some of what we need to see is already inside the box. I think I know what humans want out of life. Besides answers to natural questions, we want peace, love, enjoyment, good health, no tragedies, all that stuff. If you read the scriptures, that's what God wants, too.

Maybe the point where our wishes and God's wishes meet is our starting point. That would be a good beginning. But somehow, we need to realize that we must go beyond that, that there is a vast realm beyond our current comprehension, just waiting for us to take a shot at it. It's called the Christian journey. We must trust God's logic, even if we cannot understand it. God's logic is not a math equation waiting for us to solve. Just keep in mind, that no matter what comes down the pike, He's on our side. God's reasoning does not submit to ours, but we're told to accept His anyway. Some see that as another conflict in the human condition. Others call it faith.

Considering the fuel that motivates us to receive God's initiative, that special revelation, we cannot ignore the original question which is, "Do we need God?" We could answer this as did the gentleman in the video I watched, who simply ignored the question and expected nothing in the form of an answer from God. That line of reasoning presupposes that we would understand and already know how God might answer. However, the gospels tell us there is no human capacity for raising ourselves to God's level, so he came to ours. John's Gospel says the Word became flesh and dwelled among us. Problem is, many don't recognize it when they see it. That recognition happens only in those who have been taught to expect something from God. Question is, who's going to teach them? I believe there is an inherent need in us for something spiritual, something bigger, in our lives. But many people have been led to believe such thinking in reference to God is fantasy, unreal. They say the answer must be elsewhere. A colleague of mine called it intellectual hypocrisy. He was saying, "You're too smart to really believe that stuff." I wish I had replied, "If you're not looking for something, you won't find it." But I wasn't thinking fast enough.

This colleague of mine was an extremely bright person and an inherent over-achiever. I silently wonder sometimes, do over-achievers tend to be overly self-reliant and feel no need for Christ? Can over-achievers be dedicated Christians? These questions do not demand an answer, but they point out a human trait that goes back to original sin. The serpent said that the humans in the garden could be as good as God, implying no need for God and no need to recognize that we are not as God intended. We must somehow come to terms with that shortcoming, no matter how smart we are. As Frederick Buechner says in *Wishful Thinking, A Seeker's ABC*, "...built into the very being of even the most primitive man there seems to be a profound psychophysical need or hunger for something like truth, goodness, love, and – under one alias or another – for God;...". He goes on to say God cannot be expressed but only experienced.

To put it another way, it is one thing to *believe in* God and quite another to *believe* God. It is like looking *at* a beautiful painting or finding yourself *in* the painting. It is the difference between knowing about God and knowing God. Even the demons in the Bible knew about God.

To many of the unchurched, there is a pathway of seemingly reliable logic that discredits the existence of God. They see no evidence of Him, and they go about their daily lives with no thought of Him. They rise in the morning, carry out their daily tasks and feel they have no higher power to answer to.

There is a flip side of that logic which begins with the recognition of the enormous size and complexity of this world and this universe, and the general revelation of which we spoke of earlier. The analytical mind, if unbiased, can see that this complex world, with seasons that follow each other with predictable regularity every year for billions of years, did not happen by chance. One may say that we are learning more and more about the universe and eventually all questions will have answers. It seems, however, that the more we learn, the more we realize how much we don't know. Complex organization of nature cannot arise out of chaos without direction from a non-random higher power. I feel safe in saying that without hesitation. Once that realization sinks in, one cannot simply ignore the presence of a deity. It's a presence we cannot ignore any more than I could ignore a tiger in my living room. If we learn to believe that all things good must come from this presence, then we search for a method of recognition that is based on the concept of what is good. The enormity of God and the foundation of good must ultimately mean that, if connection is to be made, He must reach down to us out of necessity; we cannot reach Him on our own. So, we look for a spiritual venue that recognizes and appreciates His reaching down. Christianity is the only world religion that recognizes the fact that God comes to our level out of grace. Like so many questions about why this or that happens, the answers usually boil down to the fact that God took the first step.

We often find ourselves slipping into a complacent state of mind where we have small slivers of doubt about this whole "God" thing. No problem, welcome the doubt. Doubt is the seed of growth. It is precisely those moments when we must reach back to the fundamentals of our belief and realize that we have slipped because we have misplaced our faith. Our assurance of God's existence comes while doing Christ-like or God-like things with our lives, which is not our natural default behavior, and we must constantly refresh and renew it. Prayer, fellowship with other Christians, reading scripture and looking to understand it and follow it in small steps, then larger ones, make out-of-the-box logic become more and more believable. And it begins with slivers of doubt. Doubt and conflict.

Journalist Bill Tammeus, who wrote *The Value of Doubt,* made the case for, "Why unanswered questions, not unquestioned answers, build faith."[5] He openly welcomes doubt as a catalyst for growth. I say it's doubt and the conflict that comes with it. There's that word again, conflict; the human condition.

When times of God's apparent absence come to trouble you, think back to your foundations. Look for the things of your Christian discipline which brought you reassurance before and put your arms around those things in a strong embrace. It's not brainwashing yourself. The things you do for God are not imaginary. The results are ultimately clear and bear this out. God is spirit and we should not expect Him to suddenly distill out of the thin air into a visible image like a genie from a bottle just because you have slacked off on your tools of faith. But He did appear, 2000+ years ago, in the man Jesus.

As John 1:14 says, "The Word became flesh and made his dwelling among us." He came to us. He wants us to understand. What a great starting point for grappling with the human condition!

I fight with myself
I'm not sure what it all means
Maybe I'll ask God

Questions for Discussion

1. Can you think of any animal instincts we still carry, in spite of evolutionary changes, that we must keep under control?
2. Can you think of any other inner conflicts that were not mentioned?
3. If, by some method, someone is convinced that there is a God, does that obligate the person in any way to follow that God?
4. As a lay pastor, how would you answer someone who asks the question, "Why does God seem to make everything so hard?"

Notes:

1. Shirley Guthrie, Jr., Christian Doctrine, (Louisville, Westminster John Knox Press, 1994)
2. Julian Barnes, Nothing to Be Frightened Of, (New York, Alfred A. Knopf, 2008)
3. T.S. Eliot, The Cocktail Party, (Orlando, Harcourt Brace, 1950)
4. Frederick Buechner, Wishful Thinking, A Seeker's ABC, (New York, HarperCollins, 1993)
5. Bill Tammeus, The Value of Doubt, (Nashville, Skylight Paths Publishers, 2016)

Chapter Two
May I Ask Who's Calling?

One of the first of the Russian Cosmonauts to go into outer space came back with the report that he did not see God up there. He said he looked, but there was nothing there. I guess lots of folks have wondered about others who claim to be led by God. God? Where? Not sure what you're talking about.

For those of us old enough to remember, comedian Flip Wilson used to say, "The devil made me do it!" His lines were funny, no doubt, but there was also a hidden spiritual drift to some of his routines. How often we make jokes about things unseen. How much of the universe and God do we not yet understand? Astrophysicists will tell us that 95% of the universe is made of dark matter and dark energy. But they cannot tell us what it really is.

Just when we thought we had all the answers!

We may set aside time to sit and contemplate such things, and as we gain crumbs of knowledge and realization, we soon see, in all honesty, just how much we don't know.

God's people are called to various aspects of mission in Christ's community. Okay, called – by whom? Before Jesus ascended, he told us he would send someone to guide us. That someone, that third member of the Trinity showed up on the Day of Pentecost as recorded in the first part of chapter 2 in Acts of the Apostles. The world was already in the beginnings of an upheaval because of a story about a certain Jew who rose from the grave. Then, the Holy Spirit made a thundering appearance, and the world has not been the same since. But this was not the first time the Holy Spirit shows up in our Bible. Give some thought to the following scriptures:

Isaiah 61:1-4, 8-11

The spirit of the Lord God is upon me, because the Lord has anointed me; he has sent me to bring good news to the oppressed, to bind up the brokenhearted, to proclaim liberty to the captives, and release to the prisoners; ² to proclaim the year of the Lord's favor, and the day of vengeance of our God; to comfort all who mourn; ³ to provide for those who mourn in Zion— to give them a garland instead of ashes, the oil of gladness instead of mourning, the mantle of praise instead of a faint spirit. They will be called oaks of righteousness, the planting of the Lord, to display his glory.

Luke 4:16-21

When he came to Nazareth, where he had been brought up, he went to the synagogue on the sabbath day, as was his custom. He stood up to read,¹⁷ and the scroll of the prophet Isaiah was given to him. He unrolled the scroll and found the place where it was written: ¹⁸ *"The Spirit of the Lord is upon me, because he has anointed me to bring good news to the poor. He has sent me to proclaim release to the captives and recovery of sight to the blind, to let the oppressed go free, [19] to proclaim the year of the Lord's favor." [20] And he rolled up the scroll, gave it back to the attendant, and sat down. The eyes of all in the synagogue were fixed on him. [21] Then he began to say to them, "Today this scripture has been fulfilled in your hearing.*

* * * * *

I'm not sure who wrote this part of Isaiah, but the author seems like someone with an intelligent mind. It seems to be all written in implied future tense. It seems to come from having looked at the world and the direction in which it was going, from which a clear prediction arises. Clearly, this does not signal the end of a marvelous process.

Everything written in this passage is couched in positive terms. And what reinforces it more than anything is the fact that Jesus quoted these words in the synagogue of Nazareth and said that in hearing these words that day, we should consider it done, alive and well, end of story.

So, both the prophet and Jesus said, "The Spirit of the Lord is upon me." Spirit of the Lord! Let's think about that.

Too often we think of the Holy Spirit as strictly a New Testament persona. And yet here is the Old Testament prophet using that very term. That should broaden our thoughts about the Person of the Spirit.

The Holy Spirit is one of those main themes that spans both Old Testament and New Testament.

To set the stage for this discussion, let's look at a particular view of the Spirit.

In Hebrew, the word for spirit is used grammatically in feminine context. So much of our bible is written in the male gender context, but this is one subject we can see differently.

How does that help us to understand it better? Well, moms and dads are different in the minds of their children, especially small children. Dads usually represent physical strength to small children. Dads can offer heroic reassurance, comfort, and rescue, but there's just something special and endearing about a small child who climbs up into his or her mother's lap and feels safe, loved, comforted.

Think back to your very early years and remember who you sought out when you skinned your knee or needed comfort of some kind. Was it not *usually* your mother or grandmother or an aunt or a big sister? Some kind of female role figure?

In fact, the trinity has been described as the creator, redeemer, and comforter. Take a guess which one is the Spirit.

If we want to know what the Spirit is doing in our lives and in this world, we must first look at the life of Jesus and the kind of person he was and still is. The Spirit guided him practically all the time. Our search for the Holy Spirit should be Christ-centered, not self-centered. Our self-reflection should be a sincere attempt to see how we match up to the life of Jesus. That's a very high bar to reach, so be ready for a disappointment, but don't quit there. If your search for understanding the Spirit is like looking for something visible and audible like tea leaves in a cup or a rooster crowing at night, don't waste your time. All too often, we invoke the Spirit's presence to explain the trivial and unexplainable. Just because we don't have all the answers in nature doesn't mean that is where God's Spirit is. If you follow Jesus' example of living, the Spirit will be a voice, not one you hear with your ears, but a voice you can feel. The more you feel this voice, the louder it gets. But you must be paying attention. When our children are newborn, we want to listen for their cries, but it takes a focus of attention to hear that tiny voice. We must be attuned to hear God's Spirit.

We see the world around us, and we hope for something better. We ache for "feeling alive," a new life. It's that God-shaped hole you have heard about. We all have it and when it's empty, it can be the loneliest feeling in the world. The Holy Spirit fits into it perfectly and like a custom-made shoe, fills us with a sense of Christmas morning, of perfect joy, of everything in its right place and working in harmony with everything else.

Where does one find the Holy Spirit? So much has been said about it, so where is it? How do we get a foothold on this concept? Some people say they find it in themselves.

The ancient Greeks thought we had a little touch of divinity in ourselves. Therefore, in their way of thinking, to get in touch with ourselves was to get in touch with God. The problem with that is that to look for something within ourselves means we must wade through all the human messiness we carry around. It would be like looking for the game ball amid the champagne bottles and dirty towels in the winning team's locker room after a Super Bowl game.

Maybe we could ignore our personal baggage and just say the Spirit is part of our persona, part of our human nature. That's oversimplifying it to an extreme. We should not confuse or misidentify Holy Spirit with self-focus. It's not an intentional thing, but we all do it from time to time. Our soulish, unspiritual nature brings with it so many biases and self-imposed conditions and so therefore, to look for it within our own hidden private lives invariably means we will formulate something that fits our limited understanding, something that serves our convenience. Why not? Isn't that how we make most of our life choices?

Notice that both Isaiah and Jesus said, "the Spirit of the Lord is upon me." Neither man said it is inside me. It was bestowed, a gift. Neither man created it with his own thought process. Such a private religious life would not be the Holy Spirit of God. Jesus may have had private thoughts, as do we all, but his work was very public. As we love each other, the radiance of our lives, fueled by the Spirit, reflects our Lord's public work. It's like seeing someone who has a radiant confidence in doing God's work and you wonder where they get their motivation from.

It is important to know that Jesus did not invent the Holy Spirit. Our Old Testament reading today tells us that the Spirit was around long before Jesus' time on earth. The Psalms are full of direct and indirect references to the Holy Spirit.

The Holy Spirit was there when Jesus was baptized, when he was tempted in the desert, when opponents challenged him, when his followers abandoned him. It was there even when he was a young boy, talking with the elders in the temple.

In his ministry, the scriptural proclamation in Nazareth was Jesus' first sermon. It gives an example that sermons don't have to be long. He had basically stated, in unequivocal terms, who he was and what he was there to do. It was his job description and his mission statement, all rolled up into one resume. The Spirit was a major part of what he said.

This makes for a good starting point for Jesus in his ministry - and for us as we grow to understand him better.

Jesus was saying things that could be regarded as an echo of what Mary sang when she was told she would be the mother of the Messiah (Luke 1:46-55).

A portion of her song proclaims, "He has performed mighty deeds with His arm; he has scattered those who are proud in their inmost thoughts. He has brought down rulers from their thrones but has lifted up the humble. He has filled the hungry with good things but has sent the rich away empty." She said these things because she felt the Spirit's presence.

Did you ever wonder how much of her own experience Mary shared with Jesus as he was growing up? Did she tell him he was the Messiah? Did she tell him about the visit from the angel and what the angel told her? I have always wondered about that. It would have given him a great starting point, don't you think? I guess we will never know until we see God.

Okay, what kind of person was Jesus? What kind of life did he live? Look at any typical boy growing up in a blue-collar community and you probably have a good portion of that picture. There are those who would paint a picture of his life as one of constant scowling judgment, always critical, treating others with an exclusive mindset. That was not Jesus.

He loved people, all people, good folks and bad folks. He partied, ate, drank, and enjoyed joyful times. He interacted with others, talked, and listened to them as they spoke of their own lives.

Nothing is ever that easy and he was opposed from many sides because he went against the conventional thinking of those times. He claimed that what he said and did is what God says and does. He crossed to the other side of the tracks in an unprecedented manner and was a friend of sinners and loved them despite their sins. People wondered, "He's a strange one! Who does this guy think he is?" He spoke to strange women in public, something men just did not do. He had harsh words against the rich and tender words of compassion for the sick. Even the 'little' people who needed liberation were not satisfied with him. They wanted a Messiah who was a conquering hero.

The point is, following in Jesus' footsteps was not and is not an easy task. He went against the grain back then and he asks us to continue in that manner today. Get ready to be called "strange" and to find comfort in the Spirit.

In a broad perspective, we should remind ourselves that Jesus was focused on the world and others, not on himself. Our scripture from Luke makes it very clear what he was focused on. He was to bring good news to the poor. He was to proclaim release to the captives and recovery of sight to the blind, to let the oppressed go free. In many ways, his ministry started there in Nazareth.

He spoke for the poor and the rejected, defended their rights and knew when and how to prioritize personal needs of others over strict observance of the law.

The scripture speaks of the poor, the hungry, the oppressed. We may not know what that means in biblical times, but we know what it means today. The poor are not just financially poor, nor the hungry in need of just food. The oppressed could be those enslaved or those denied opportunities to find happiness in this life.

Captive? Are any of us captive to anything? Fear? Doubt? Anger? Is your life as whole as you want it to be? What kind of invisible prison bars surround you? Do you instinctively avoid certain things or people because of painful memories, painful grudges, regrets?

Yes, I think we can relate to what Isaiah and Jesus were saying. We've seen it. We have seen the oppressed and the blind and we've looked the other way. Is the Holy Spirit upon us or only on Isaiah and Jesus?

Jesus loved his enemies. That's a hard one. I've known some real arrogant donkeys in my life, some who got what they wanted by walking over others, sometimes over me. I sat down one day and began listing those who have wronged me, a mental list. What would I say to them if they walked into my house? The more I thought of the past, the angrier I got and the more distant from God I felt. The Spirit knows the biggest common denominator we have with those whom we regard as enemies is our own human weakness, the conflicts, the human condition we discussed in the previous chapter. The Spirit brings us to the reality of God's love.

Jesus was just as human as you and me, yet he never lost his trust in God, even when he felt abandoned.

He was led, inspired, and empowered by the Holy Spirit in everything he did. As we examine his life to emulate it, we should pay attention to what empowered him. He gave the source of empowerment to us. Sometimes I think that was like giving the keys from the family car to a ten-year-old. But that's what he did.

So, going forward, we live in a timeframe between Jesus' time on earth and the time when he will come again. How do we fit into this timeframe? What do we do with the time God has given us?

We should be wondering what we need to do in order to allow God's transformation to happen in us and in the world. Are we like the artist who is constantly looking for ways to improve his talent? Or do we let the distractions of the world speak louder than Isaiah's words of truth?

Today true spirituality is based on the memory and belief of Jesus' resurrection and what God has done in the past. That memory assures us of what God will do in the future. That assurance is so very comforting, and the Spirit brings it to us.

As the Spirit inspires us to follow Jesus' example, we must first look outside ourselves, beyond our personal experiences, and then we know what to look for on the inside. This is why learning scripture is so important. That is where we learn about Jesus' life. That is where we find the template on which to base our spirituality. That is where we will find clues to answers.

The work of the Spirit can be found in ordinary, everyday human experience in which there is perhaps no apparent supernatural intervention. It is the same Spirit today as it was in Jesus' time.

God's Spirit is free to blow wherever God wills. It works among believers and non-believers. In fact, we should not lead ourselves into thinking that the Holy Spirit is trapped inside the church.

It can be seen and felt in both good times and bad. Our spirituality is not based on just "success stories."

True spirituality is that of Christians who know that the Holy Spirit does not always save us from our weaknesses but helps us in our weak moments to give us comfort, strength, and faith. The Holy Spirit helps us remember that, as Paul said, nothing can separate us from the love of God.

So, it sounds like God has a plan; a plan that goes back many centuries, maybe even to creation. We are part of that plan, you and me.

This is a time of waiting and preparing for God to transform the world through the life of Jesus. The words of Isaiah tell us that this transformation is not an empty hope, but a sure promise.

Every baby born starts off with an investment account from God. He has signed it and we grow with compound interest. No one has ever reached an upper limit of that growth. Let the power and reality of the Holy Spirit, the great comforter, embrace us in the everlasting arms, give us warmth and courage, and bring out our genuine humanness – and watch it grow.

Every new Commissioned Pastor should surrender to the Holy Spirit. Surrender, but use the brains and the heart God gave you.

> I'm in the starting gate,
> From here I can't see the finish.
> Just follow the track.

Questions for Discussion

1. When the Holy Spirit speaks to you, how do you know it is the Spirit talking and not just your juices flowing?
2. What evidence can you find in scripture that the Trinity already existed at the time of creation?
3. What obstacles can you think of that prevents us from a meaningful conversation with the Holy Spirit?

Chapter Three
God's Mailbox

As I stated in the introduction, Philip Yancey is one of my favorite authors and I derive much of my sermon material from his words. For example, this chapter was once a sermon I preached making use of inspiration from his book, *Prayer*. I recommend it highly. I have adapted that sermon for this chapter.

So, you find yourself starting a journey, a spiritual journey. In order to know the way, you need one of two things, a map, or a guide. The Christian journey gives you both because they both complement each other. In fact, they require each other. The map is the scriptures, and the guide is the One on the other end of your prayers. To successfully read the map, must one adopt the mindset of Dr. Indiana Jones as he looks at ancient symbols and hieroglyphics? No, wait – it's not that complicated. But we must remember that the scriptures were not written with 21st century audiences in mind. The Bible, especially the Old Testament, was written for an audience of really ancient Hebrews. Really ancient, like *really old*. They had their own way of communicating and placing emphasis where it was needed.

But God is not limited to the idioms and phrases of ancient Hebrews. He hears us just as well today as He did thousands of years ago. Human languages may have changed but human nature and human needs have not. The scriptural map verifies this. It tells us that we have an open microphone to God, as long as we remember the love, wisdom, and power of God.

Psalms 145:17-19 tells us: *^{17}The Lord is just in all his ways, and kind in all his doings. ^{18}The Lord is near to all who call on him, to all who call on him in truth. ^{19}He fulfills the desire of all who fear him; he also hears their cry and saves them.*

He knows our needs and we connect with Him when we tell Him what He already knows. Philippians 4:6-7 tells us:

^{6}Do not worry about anything, but in everything by prayer and supplication with thanksgiving let your requests be made known to God. ^{7}And the peace of God, which surpasses all understanding, will guard your hearts and your minds in Christ Jesus.

Something that has always given me reason to pause and pinch myself is when Jesus talked about asking - in his name. John 14:13-14 says it plain as day:

^{13}I will do whatever you ask in my name, so that the Father may be glorified in the Son. ^{14}If in my name you ask me for anything, I will do it.

How cool is that? All I must do is add a little phrase at the end about asking in his name and that's it? It's that simple and yet, it's that complicated. "In his name" is just the tip of the iceberg.

The question for the day is this, "Why do we pray?" Can you imagine what kind of relationship would exist in a marriage where two partners didn't talk to each other? What if one partner talked but the other refused to answer?

Prayer is the primary thing that nourishes our relationship with God. This is basic, fundamental stuff. Something we should all feel the need for.

When Einstein was once asked about future research, he said, "Find out about prayer. Someone must find out about prayer."

Back in the late 80's, there was a movie, "Let It Ride." - The previews showed Richard Dreyfuss at the racetrack on his knees praying. A later scene in the movie had him throwing money in the air and saying "God likes me! He really, really likes me!" Do we do that? Do you feel closer to God, blessed, when your 401K goes up? Do we send up a request and then dream up associations between events, connect the dots and tell ourselves that must be the answer? Do we look for signs? Do we feel closer to God because our prayers were answered when we found a parking place, or the light changed so we wouldn't be late for an appointment?

Do we regard prayer as something we send from the visible world into the invisible world like an email in hopes that someone will receive it?

Do we use prayer as a good luck charm? Remember years ago, the song about the hot-rod Lincoln by Charlie Ryan? One of the lines had these words: "Topped a hill, passed a truck, whispered a prayer just for luck." When we do that, we regard prayer as a form of transaction. We say, "I prayed this, now you have to do that."

We humans want so badly to take complex issues and make them simple. I wonder why? Is it so we can understand it better? Maybe we want to reduce something complicated down to its lowest common denominator so we can put it on the shelf and not having it hanging over our heads. We do that with God all the time.

Philip Yancey interviewed many people to find out what they thought about prayer.[2] He got all kinds of answers, but all too many said they didn't really find it satisfying. They rarely felt the presence of God. Yancey said he encountered a huge gap between the theory of prayer and the practice of prayer.

Advances in technology confuse our feelings about prayer. In centuries past, farmers prayed for rain and today they watch the Weather Channel and work with their irrigation systems. We used to cry out to God when a child fell ill. Now we pick up the phone. In developing third world countries people spend little time wondering about prayer and more time actually praying. Prosperity dilutes prayer. How can you pray for daily bread when your pantry is fully stocked?

We are all so involved in our attempts to control things around us, we forget to follow what Psalm 46 tells us - *be still and know that I am God.* We are called upon to stop what we are doing, put down our tools and thoughts about this world, take a mental vacation, and know the enormity of God. Our planet is just a small speck of dust in the cosmos, and we are just dots, almost invisible dots on that speck of dust. This universe is still a place of mystery.

Einstein was right. We need to learn about prayer. How do we learn to pray? Simple answer, we learn to pray by praying. As Yancey put it, a child learns to talk by imitating the parent who speaks to him in a language he doesn't understand yet. Prayer is where God and humankind meet, and it involves two questions: Why doesn't God act the way I want him to and why don't I act the way God wants me to? Prayer is where those two questions come together.

How much are your prayers about you and how much are about God? We need to understand what God wants from us more than what we want from God. No matter what you may think your needs are, your greatest need is a personal encounter with God. Maybe you think it is useless just to pray about God when there is so much you need to ask for. Get closer to God, and just maybe your requests will start sounding like God's requests. The result of prayer tells us who and what God is as well as what God wants, from running your life to running an entire church. Prayer is where you encounter God; not just sitting in a pew and listening to someone else preaching from a pulpit.

So, let's go a little deeper into this. In order to approach God in prayer, we must come to him just as we are. How often do we go to God in prayer without bringing out our inner self? Without admitting how helpless we really are? Pretending we have no faults? Bringing your ego into prayer is like hitting a brick wall. You're just talking into the wind, with no one listening. Father Henri Nouwen said we should always take the stance that we are human, and God is God. When you truly do that, the conversation with God begins. It is a humbling experience, and we will not connect to God if we are too proud to be humbled. God wants us to be our authentic self, just as we are. It is so liberating to know that God encourages me to face my dark side in my prayers. Know that you can trust God with your secrets because He already knows them.

Try this. You know your own faults. Close your eyes and mentally list them. All the untruths, the way you may have dehumanized others, insincerities in relationships, taking what was not yours, violating promises – keep going, there's so much more that you keep buried. Exhaust your list and then picture someone who knows about everything on that list. Now face the fact that the list is real and so is that person who knows all your secrets.

Now, you're ready to pray.

Prayer is the gift of the Spirit. We are empowered to pray because God gave us the ability. Often, we wonder how to pray, when to pray, what to pray. We can become very concerned about methods and techniques of prayer. Truthfully, it is not we who pray but the Spirit who prays in us.

Paul says (Romans 8:26-27): *"The Spirit ... comes to help us in our weakness, for when we do not know how to pray properly, then the Spirit personally makes our petitions for us in groans that cannot be put into words; and he who can see into all hearts knows what the Spirit means because the prayers that the Spirit makes for*

God's holy people are always in accordance with the mind of God". These words explain why the Spirit is often called "the Consoler."

Don't worry about having the right words. God hears more than just words. He hears what you feel and think. He knows the deepest parts of you that you never make known to others. With casual friends, we reveal and discuss casual things. The deeper the topics become, the deeper the friendship. How deep is your relationship to God? You want to really talk with God? Don't hold anything back. He wants the real you, not something you place before him like a billboard that says, "Here I am, this is all you get!" And yet we want Him to reveal all of Himself to us. What hypocrisy we try to sell! We must trust God with what He already knows. Ever see a person putting up the front of doing something wonderful and generous when all along you know how rotten he really is? You say defiantly to yourself, "You don't fool me! I know who you really are." Could God see us with such defiance? Not really, He forgives. But He could. You're not fooling Him.

Father Henri Nouwen said the paradox of prayer is that it requires a serious effort on our part while at the same time the ability to pray can only be received as a gift. Our prayers cannot organize, plan, or manipulate God; but without a straightforward and honest approach, we cannot receive Him either.

I spoke earlier about prayer requests. Is it wrong to go to the Father with requests? If we are following Jesus' example, remember His prayer in the garden. It was all requests. But it was all put in the context of working within God's will. We do not tell God things he does not already know. We don't remind Him of things he has forgotten. He is simply waiting for us to care about things He cares about already. Jesus says He no longer calls us servants, because a servant does not know the master's business. Instead, He calls us friends because He has passed on to us everything the Father passed to him. We must know the master's business. We should be in a partnership, a tight friendship bound with prayer, because prayer is the language of that friendship. As Yancey says, that partnership should be so tight we can't see who is doing what, God or the human partner. We should ask God to show us what He is doing today and tells us how we can be part of it.

John 15:7 says: *"If you abide in me and my words abide in you, ask what you will, and it will be given to you."* What does it mean to abide in Christ? It is said that a weak person who has fallen into temptation but is strengthened and upheld by a friend must maintain contact with his friend. Otherwise, he will fall back into his old ways. His safety depends on continual contact with his friend. Abiding in Christ means staying in contact with Him. You must do it deliberately. Like all relationships, it requires work. Arrange your life around time for prayer.

How many of us are Red Sox fans? How many of us have been to Fenway? If not, think of some other team or some other favorite venue. Imagine the last time you went. If you went with someone, you probably shared the feelings of excitement when you saw the crowds, when you walked up the entrance ramp and caught your first glimpse of the field, when you saw the players come out. Can you remember what the crowd sounded like? Chances are, everyone was on about the same page. So, maybe you went by yourself. Did that diminish the enjoyment somewhat? It would for me. What if the people sitting around you were busy talking about food, cars, or their last trip to the doctor? Would you be distracted? Maybe. What a blessing to have someone with you who is seeing the same thing, sharing the same feelings. Does prayer do that for us? Should we ask God to help us see what He is seeing? Try this; next time you have a request for God, try to envision why the request is needed. Look into the background and see why it matters to you. Maybe that 'why' would put you closer to what God sees rather than the request itself. When I worked for the State of Florida several years ago, we had an administrator who knew how to get to the bottom of any negotiation. Someone would say, "We need to buy this piece of equipment." Or "We need to implement this certain policy." He would say "Why?" Someone would give an explanation and he would repeat, "Why?" So that put us at a different level, perhaps one layer away from the original suggestion. So, someone else would offer a response that was yet another layer away. The 'why' would come again. Soon, he would have us realizing why we really wanted the original request and often it turned out that what we needed was something entirely different. Well, this fellow wasn't God, but we can approach God the same way. If we ask and don't get what we want, ask why. Ask yourself what do I really need? Ask why your request doesn't fit God's will. Talk to God, really talk to Him. Keep asking why and build on the answer you get. Hopefully, you and God will soon be looking at the same thing.

What about requests that are not granted? We ask for an end to hunger, end to war, better lives for others. Yes, God wants that, too. So many tragedies are because people make the evil choice or the wrong choice. It's why the holocaust happened and why there is war in Ukraine. Life is a symphony. God is the composer. Christ is the conductor. The Holy Spirit brings the musicians together in harmony with the composer. But some don't listen to the melody. They play their own version, use their own rhythm. The brokenness of this world is because of bad choices by people. But do we ask why did God not prevent the earthquake, the tidal wave, the volcano? These are things over which we have no direct control and are not, from what we can tell, the result of human sinfulness.

Why do they happen? I don't have a clue! I have no answer for you as to why God lets these things happen, but He does want us to talk to Him about them. Yes, show our anger for letting these things happen. But always ask for help to see it the way He sees it. Someone of weak faith may say, "How could a powerful God allow something like this to happen?" I don't know the correct answer. But I know what the incorrect answer sounds like. It's not because God has stopped loving us! One of the greatest themes in the Bible is that God identifies with suffering. If you doubt it, just look at the cross. In a world of pain, how could we worship a God who is immune to pain? God wants you to be a candle in a dark room. And no, I don't know why the room is dark! Someday when I see God, I'll ask Him why.

I don't think God would make it so just so we would have something to pray about! But my instructions are clear! And so are yours.

Should we wrestle with God? You bet! Tell Him your disappointment. If you hate something, tell Him! Demand an explanation! God is big enough to take your anger and He knows that sometimes anger is needed to get it all out where you can see it. Be angry but ask for understanding. Always try to see it through His eyes. The Bible is full of protests being lifted up to God telling Him that justice and mercy do not rule the earth. So, in your anger, know that you are in the company of the prophets. They were angry, just like you. But their faith endured. Ask God to keep your faith in Him alive.

Speaking of anger, sometimes my anger is because of a spiritual dry spell. I sometimes have the sense that no one is listening on the other end. A book I read about Mother Teresa said that she had a dry spell that lasted for years.

Periods of spiritual dryness, in which we wonder where God disappeared to, can be expected. Even God's human incarnation was not exempt. We instinctively blame ourselves. Should we stop praying when this happens? If we do, how will we know when prayer becomes alive again? We should examine our motives for praying. Perhaps we are seeking God on our terms.

Rest assured that God cares for us more than we care for ourselves. He does not play guessing games with us. If the dryness we feel is because of some failing on our part, He will make it clear to us. Keep praying! Don't toy with vague doubts. Clear your mind and listen for His small, still voice.

Christ simply asked that we give him our ALL. Give Him your whole self and He will give you a new self. The hard part is handing yourself over to him, but then the new self is the easy part, the happy part. You won't have to worry about doing the right thing; it will be part of your spiritual self and you won't have to give up any part of it to be happy.

One of my best friends was Pastor Rick Underwood. Not just my friend, he was my pastor when we lived in Massachusetts. His depth of thought was something I always admired and set up as my standard to work toward. One day we were discussing the essence of prayer and he told me I should picture a conversation that is ongoing within the Trinity. Not a human conversation, but a conversation, nonetheless. Prayer, he said, is our attempt to become part of that conversation. Get in touch with God, he told me. God already knows what you need. Rick passed into God's hands a few years back. I miss our conversations over lunch.

How do we find the strength and courage to be part of that holy conversation? By communicating with God through prayer. Pray and listen. That's when we will look at God and the world in a different way. That bad dream you've been living will be over and it will be the most beautiful morning of your life.

So, when people ask you the question I posed in the beginning, "Why do you pray?", the best answer a Christian can give is, "Because

Jesus prayed." He stayed in touch with the Father and there's no better example to follow.

If God in Jesus is not the main issue in your life, talk to Him. Remember, He's already there and ready to listen. Look at the map, talk to the guide and start the journey.

I have His number.
There is so much to ask Him.
Hello! Are You there?

Questions for Discussion

1. If God already knows our needs and our thoughts, why do we need to pray to Him?
2. If someone you know has lost a child to illness despite many prayers, how do you answer if they claim that God was not listening?
3. What good does it do to recite memorized prayers?

Notes:

1. Philip Yancey, Prayer, (Grand Rapids, Zondervan, 2006)
2. Ibid.

Chapter Four

Faith or Belief or Imagination

Hebrews 11:1-6

11Now faith is the assurance of things hoped for, the conviction of things not seen. Indeed, by faith our ancestors received approval. By faith we understand that the worlds were prepared by the word of God, so that what is seen was made from things that are not visible.

By faith Abel offered to God a more acceptable sacrifice than Cain's. Through this he received approval as righteous, God himself giving approval to his gifts; he died, but through his faith he still speaks. By faith Enoch was taken so that he did not experience death; and "he was not found, because God had taken him." For it was attested before he was taken away that "he had pleased God." And without faith it is impossible to please God, for whoever would approach him must believe that he exists and that he rewards those who seek him.

* * * * *

There are many things about the Bible that I do not understand, so I focus on those things which seem to repeat themselves, because they must be important. One of those things is love. Another is faith. Did you know that in the letters to the Romans and Hebrews, the word 'Faith' is used more than 30 times in each book? In fact, if you have a fairly large Bible concordance, you will see that the NIV translation of the New Testament mentions 'Faith' 249 times. There must be something important about it. We hear that Jesus would so often say, "Your faith has made you whole." Sounds like self-healing. Surely not. So, what is faith? It's one of those things that sometime seem abstract and which I must constantly re-define in my own thoughts, not so much as to what the dictionary says, but my mind wants to know how it works?

The best definition of faith is from the book of Hebrews, chapter 11, verse 1. The King James version says, "Now faith is the substance of things hoped for, the evidence of things not seen." The NIV Bible says, "Now faith is being sure of what we hope for, and certain of what we do not see."

When we read scripture, it is not like an owner's manual that shows us how to assemble something. If the parts are right there and the instructions are clearly printed and readable, who needs imagination? When we moved to Virginia, the value of IKEA stock went up, I'm sure. We bought about a dozen items from that store, all of which had to be put together. IKEA does a great job of illustrating their assembly directions. No imagination needed.

Try doing that with scripture, any scripture!

But how much of scripture interpretation requires our imagination in order to come to an understanding of it?

In the whole equation of salvation, if you will allow me to use that term, God gives us many things. He gives us grace, forgiveness, sacrifice, love, and on and on. But everything He requires of us starts with one thing, and that is faith. Faith is our contribution to the equation. Without it, the plan is incomplete. Hebrews 11:6 tells us that without faith, we cannot please God. Faith is the believer stepping up to the plate and swinging at the first pitch. All faith must have a basis, a reason to have it. That reason is God's gift to us. But this gift from God doesn't come with an obvious bow and ribbon, in plain sight to be scooped up and opened. There must be sufficient reason to see it for what it is and to use it as a basis of your faith, a starting point. Imagination is like a blank check. You can make it whatever you want it to be. If we are not careful, we use imagination to form ridiculous images in our mind and then try to attach reality to them. Used properly, imagination fills in the blanks and then we go about testing what we have filled in, like writing a term paper and then reviewing and editing. But how do we find that starting point?

When I was in graduate school, I was taking a course in biostatistics, and we had been given a homework assignment over a weekend. Math is not my strongest weapon and come Monday, the professor asked for volunteers to go to the board and write out the assignment for the class to discuss. No way was I going to raise my hand. He paused for a nanosecond and said, "Okay, Slayter – go to the board."

It only took me a few seconds to write it out and I turned to him and smiled weakly. I was sure there was something I had left out. So, he asked me to state the point of the exercise and I began with, "Well, this proves..." And he stopped me.

"You haven't proven anything," he said.

So, I tried a different approach. I said, "This shows that..." And he stopped me again. "Doesn't show anything," he said.

I tried a couple of other attempts with the same result and finally laid the chalk down and said, "Okay, you tell me what's what." I was the oldest in the class, about the same age as the professor and I was tired and not ready to play guessing games with this arrogant swellhead.

He walked to the head of the room with a bit of a swagger and said, "What we have here is sufficient evidence to behave as though we believe a certain thing to be true."

No one made a sound. This was supposed to be a math class and he made it sound like a theology lecture.

Sufficient evidence to behave as though we believe a certain thing to be true. That was over 40 years ago, and I still remember it verbatim. He was talking about a basis for faith. Not bad for a swellhead.

The word faith is misconstrued many times. When a person fills out an application for something or when a recruit joins the military, he or she may be asked, "What is your religious faith?"

Faith is not religion. Faith is not our denomination. Faith is not simply agreeing with a collection of thoughts that seem to connect the dots in a logical way. We cannot say, "This makes sense and therefore that makes sense. Isn't that nice." Faith is belief that leads to a change in us. It would be hard to find a worldly example to compare to faith in God, but let's try. I have faith in the sunrise because I have seen it happen. Faith in God is more than that. I have faith that people sitting out there in the pews are not an illusion because I can see them. Faith in God is more than that. Like our reading from Hebrews at the beginning of this chapter, faith is being sure of what we hope for and certain of what we cannot see.

Belief and faith are two different things. In James 2:19 we read, *"You believe that there is one God. Good - even the demons believe this, and shudder."* They have no loving confidence in God.

Faith is not just trying to believe. The word 'trying' means there is an element of doubt, possible failure. Even Yoda told Luke Skywalker as much in the second Star Wars movie. Faith is to believe so strongly that you confidently base all your actions on what you believe.

In his book, *Jesus is the Question,*[1] Martin Copenhaver uses the example of a circus ringmaster introducing a famous high-wire artist. He asks the crowd how many believe this man can ride safely over the high wire on a bicycle with someone else on his shoulders. There was a tremendous wave of hands showing their belief. The ringmaster then asked who in the crowd would be the first volunteer to sit on the man's shoulders. Guess how many raised their hand?

Faith is not about believing; it is about trust.

Faith is not intellectual. Faith in God comes from the heart.

Faith is not hope alone. Hope is our spiritual anchor. Faith is the mechanism whereby we see hope as a reality. Without hope, there can be no faith. But God gives us hope. **There are different kinds of hope.** Some hope is just wishful thinking. Faith comes from hope that is utterly convinced, despite things to the contrary.

Faith is the spiritual force through which your ministry for Christ becomes effective. It is the major key to success.

Can you develop faith? Certainly. God has given each of us the ability to develop faith. In fact, faith itself is a gift in the first place! (1Cor 12:4, 9, 31; 13:13). Listen to the Word of God; learn from it. Seek to do what is holy. Paul tells us to pray continuously. That means having God on your mind, running in the background all day. Obey the guidance of the Holy Spirit and use whatever gifts God has given you and that includes imagination. Remember that Christianity is a journey. Do what you are called to do today, for tomorrow there will be more adventure. Give thanks for what you have today. Realize that our relationship with one another is a key element of Christianity. And remember that Jesus said anything we ask for in his name will be granted. When your faith is strong enough to see glimmers of God's will and what you ask for is in his name, his will, the results will stagger you. Remember the first time you went off a high diving board? You went to the edge, looked over, began your jump, and I don't know about you, but my thought was, "Oh my God, this is really happening." Seeing God in action is a rush that has no comparison.

But let us not get caught up in thinking that faith is all there is. Maybe we should not try to isolate faith as a single circumscribed entity. That would be like picking a leaf from a tree and using it to try to figure out how the whole tree functions. Faith is in the background of just about everything we do in our relationship with God. It is the third rail that keeps the train powered and moving. Maybe we should not worry about trying to dissect it into parts; just know it's there and we need it to keep on track with our Christian journey.

We could cope - the world could cope - with a Jesus who ultimately remains just a wonderful idea inside his disciples' minds and hearts. But the world cannot cope with a Jesus who comes out of the tomb, who inaugurates God's creation right in the middle of the old one.

We've got an empty tomb and disciples behaving like something really great has happened. How does history deal with this? In science, when a conclusion doesn't fit the context of the experiment, what do we do? We either throw out the results or we widen the context.

It was Picasso who said, "Every child is an artist. The problem is how to remain an artist when we grow up." Imagination is the force that trespasses on the impossible. For children, imagining is an easy task, but as we age that force lies muffled. Not replaced or destroyed, but muffled.

Imagination is crucial to our faith, not because it conjures up images of fairy tales, but because it opens our minds to possibilities that do not fit into the logical world as we see it. Faith and imagination need each other equally in this Christian life.

In today's culture, we are either too passive or too lazy for such thinking and we allow culture and society to do our imagining for us. Culture is constantly telling us what should be. We say, "Beef. It's what for dinner!" or "What happens in Vegas stays in Vegas!" These are cultural invitations to imagine what could be. So much of the media does this for us. It may be that imagination is a treasure for ordinary people who dare not lose it, but it is even more tragically sad for a Christian to lose it.

There is an interplay between imagination and faith. Imagination is the ability to visualize what is not visual. That is, seeing the unseeable. We do it in business all the time. We call it casting a vision. You could call it a form of art. Art is always imagination because it makes visible what is hard to believe. It can be upsetting because it crosses the line between abstract and what we can hold with our hands.

Logic may change your mind, but the interplay between imagination and faith changes your life. Imagination visualizes what faith knows to be true. Then it becomes a belief. If imagination were a kite, factual faith is the string connecting it to the handler. Again, Hebrews 11:1 says, "Faith is the confidence that what we hope for will actually happen; it gives us assurance about things we cannot see."

Without the faith connection, a theological connection, the kite is tossed about, and imagination is out of control. Faith accompanied by imagination is so much more than delusion and myth. It is faith that calls us to imagine, but to imagine with biblically correct assurance. With that assurance, imagination then becomes a reality, and we call it belief.

Our imagination allows us to accept in faith something that works even though our intellect cannot explain how it does. The other element required by the Christian faith is the ability to believe an event that is impossible through solely natural means. The Bible tells us that with God all things are possible. It would be wise to not go overboard with that. Fantasy is not part of the equation, but it stands close by.

Christians are called to imagine what could be and what will be, while also living in the present. For example, as Kingdom's citizens, it's a calling to see people as the object of love, not as enemies. That happens only when our imagination is biblically developed.

It is a calling to action, not spectatorship. James 2:16 tells us if one sees a man cold, hungry, and naked and says, "Keep warm and eat well," then faith is nothing. Faith in God must have action.

It's like saying, "Have a nice day!" It costs us nothing.

Samuel Wells, author of *Humbler Faith, Bigger God*,[2] says that God is an essence, that is, a quality of being. An essence, by its very nature is timeless, and therefore, forever. By contrast, we humans are an existence, something of finite features. As an existence, we are endowed with the ability to envision something bigger, higher, infinitely more complex than we are. Sensing such presence, we seek to know it better and it is by faith that we continue to search and believe in our efforts. By virtue of our faith, we admit that there is something more to discover. That faith comes into play in all that we do while we are in the embrace of God.

Logic tells us there are different kinds of hope. Some hope is just wishful thinking. Faith comes from hope that is utterly convinced. It's the kind of hope we read about in Hebrews 11:1.

So, is faith one of the pretty ornaments on the tree of Christianity? Is it some decorative ancillary aspect like using the right liturgical colors according to the calendar? Does it enhance discussions of Christian theology like a manger scene enhances Christmas décor? Faith is like oxygen to our living tissues, like sunlight to a field of growing wheat. According to Dr. Shirley Guthrie in his book, *Christian Doctrine*,[3] "If it could be said that the whole of the Christian faith stands or falls with any one claim, the claim that God raised the crucified Jesus from the dead is that claim. Without faith in a risen and living Christ there would be no Christianity. It was not Jesus' ethical teachings and example or his noble death that gave birth to the Christian Church and made it spread; it was the news of his resurrection."

Indeed, without faith in the resurrection, all we would have is a dead body and a sad story of a murder. If you have faith in the resurrection, what's stopping you from having faith in everything else Jesus taught us?

> What's that you tell me?
> It's too good to not be true.
> Sounds good. Tell me more.

Questions for Discussion

1. What is your basis for faith?
2. Is everyone's basis the same?
3. If you peel back the layers of your faith, assuming each layer is because of a deeper layer, what is the final layer for which there is no 'because' beyond it?

Notes:

1. Martin Copenhaver, *Jesus is the Question,* (Nashville, Abingdon Press, 2014)
2. Samuel Wells, *Humbler Faith, Bigger God,* (Grand Rapids, Eerdmans Publishing, 2022)
3. Shirley Guthrie, Jr., *Christian Doctrine,* (Louisville, Westminster John Knox Press, 1994)

Chapter Five

Ambassadors of the Kingdom

Matthew 22:15-22

[15]Then the Pharisees went and plotted to entrap him in what he said.[16]So they sent their disciples to him, along with the Herodians, saying, "Teacher, we know that you are sincere, and teach the way of God in accordance with truth, and show deference to no one; for you do not regard people with partiality.[17]Tell us, then, what you think. Is it lawful to pay taxes to the emperor, or not?"[18]But Jesus, aware of their malice, said, "Why are you putting me to the test, you hypocrites?[19]Show me the coin used for the tax." And they brought him a denarius.[20]Then he said to them, "Whose head is this, and whose title?"[21]They answered, "The emperor's." Then he said to them, "Give therefore to the emperor the things that are the emperor's, and to God the things that are God's."[22]When they heard this, they were amazed; and they left him and went away.

* * * * *

This particular scripture carries forward two questions: what belongs to the emperor and what belongs to God? The answer to the first question is obvious, but the second question requires some thought. Once we arrive at what appears to be the correct thought for that second question, what must we do with that information?

Jesus had made quite the scene on several occasions throughout Galilee and into Judea. So, let's set the stage for this encounter between Jesus and the prevailing playground bullies. I use the word 'bullies' for a reason. Notice that the Pharisees did not approach Jesus themselves, they sent their disciples. What cowards!!

In verses leading up to this conversation, Jesus' authority was being questioned by the Pharisees and he answered them with his own question: by what authority was John baptizing? When they could not answer honestly, Jesus proceeded to utter a series of parables, starting with the parable of the two sons, then the parable of the tenants, and finally the wedding parable.

In each parable, the Pharisees were the villains. The Pharisees knew the point he was making, although they could not admit it for fear of losing their own credibility. So, they teamed up with supporters of Herod and attempted another entrapment. Even though Herodians and temple officials may have had huge differences, Jesus was their common enemy, so the scripture says that both factions were present in this plot to trap Jesus. Notice how Jesus does not try to use some kind of tangible, symbolic, material evidence to make his point. His point lies in the hearts of those who hear him.

Notice how the Pharisees first lavished him with shallow flattery. How many of you have been approached by someone who sings your praises first before asking you for something? The intent, we assume here, is to make the wanted answer obvious and the unwanted answer awkward. Stacking the deck, we would say.

Not only that, but they also approached him in a public venue so his response would be undeniable.

Let's talk a minute about these two groups who opposed Jesus.

Jewish high society was divided into two factions represented by Herodians, who supported King Herod Antipas, a king who was on the throne by Roman approval, and the Sanhedrin of the temple, who lived by Jewish law.

We must remember that the Jews lived in constant awareness of the broad shadow cast by Rome. There might be squabbles among themselves, but as long as there was no threat to the authority of Rome, the Romans let them bicker and argue like 5-year-old siblings.

The tax question, however, carried a crucial implication. Jesus was being asked to choose between Jewish law and Roman law. Either way, it was a pitfall and Jesus knew it.

Jesus had a great deal of insight into the minds of people. It's called emotional intelligence. Hear the words from John 2:25: "He did not need man's testimony about man, for he knew what was in a man."

So, here's his choice: If he showed disdain for paying tribute to Rome, he could be accused of insurrection and treason. If he said it was lawful to pay the taxes that Rome imposed, he would discredit himself in the eyes of many and scandalize the Jewish religious establishment, the very institution to which he was trying to bring the good news.

Jesus' previous defiance of temple authority gave his opponents reason to believe he was close to being a revolutionary. Such rebellious behavior by other groups had had disastrous results two decades earlier.

One of Jesus' most used tactics was to take such a question and throw it back in the laps of those who posed it. Jewish rabbis were well known for answering a question with a question. Jesus had a habit of speaking the truth in love, words Paul would later use in his letter to the Ephesians.

Jesus often replied to people with gentleness and finesse, but this time, he was as subtle as a freight train. He knew he was being set up and he spoke the truth assertively when he said, "Why are you putting me to the test, you hypocrites?"

His response to their plot made use of what was obvious. The control of society, the infrastructure of the countryside, came from the taxes paid to Rome. Rome was brutal, but it did provide some form of stability to Israel. Anyone on the street could see that.

Let's talk about that coin for a minute.

Coins that were minted locally were copper. Only Rome could mint coinage in silver and gold, and these were the coins used to pay taxes to Caesar and they were inscribed with the word, 'Divine' to describe Caesar. Romans considered Caesar to be a deity, a god. So, was paying tribute to him a violation of the first two commandments?

The first says, "You shall have no other god before me." The second condemned any kind of graven image to be worshipped. And here is a coin with Caesar's likeness on it and the word 'divine.'

So, Jesus used the obvious to make his point. What belonged to Caesar was clearly evident, so let him have what was his. He continued, "...and to God what is God's." But what belonged to God? He didn't say. Maybe there was wisdom in Jesus' answer in the fact that he did not reveal a similar object or trinket to say, "This belongs to God."

Where was the counterpart to the Roman coin? Where was the symbol of what belonged to God? Maybe Jesus was referring to the Kingdom of heaven. Without a doubt, that belongs to God.

Jesus' teachings, his sermons, his parables, all described the kingdom of Heaven in an indirect manner. How many times did we read his words, "The Kingdom of Heaven is like....."

Maybe the Kingdom of Heaven was not so simple that it could be boiled down to a handful of words that sounded like, "The Kingdom of Heaven is THIS, or the Kingdom of Heaven is THAT...". Maybe it was beyond what human words could convey.

Maybe it still is.

That same math professor I mentioned in the previous chapter introduced me to a word that has an impact in areas outside of mathematics. The word is asymptotic. It means two lines coming closer and closer to each other, but never touching – even out to infinity.

Our understanding of God's Kingdom has an asymptotic relationship with the true nature of God's Kingdom. During this life on earth, we can come closer and closer to understanding the Kingdom, but we will never know the total truth. Not in this life. We accept this fact by faith.

Jesus did not want to reduce God's Kingdom to a few paltry words that people would memorize and then lose their meaning.

Sometimes I think we do that. Creeds and confessions – how many have we memorized? How often do we recite them from rote memory without really thinking about their meaning and impact?

One of the main messages of Jesus' encounter over the coin is that we have a working ability to discern what belongs to God's. We must act on that discernment.

To be human is to be offered a significant choice. We may choose to open ourselves to God thru Christ, to speak and act as the image of God. Or we may choose not to.

There's that word again: image.

So, we have the image of Caesar on the coin. What carries God's image?

Look around you. The streets, the stores, the churches, the homes are filled with God's image. The Kingdom of God is within you (Luke 17:21) and is God's gift that makes us human and in His image.

In the ancient world, an image was believed to carry the essence of that which created it. The governing work of God was accomplished by the people He created. To be in his image provides the capacity not only to serve as His representative, but to be and act like Him. The tools He gave us to accomplish that task include conscience, self-awareness, and spiritual discernment. One could probably write a whole book on the topic of being in God's image, because that's what we are. We are special.

It is through Jesus that we are called to be more truly human, reflecting the image of God into the world. The more we reflect that image, the more human we become.

The Bible, through scripture, helps us to see that as God works within his world, he does it through his image-bearing human creatures by communicating with them to the extent that their intellect will allow.

Think of all the things God has accomplished by inspiring and motivating someone, somewhere, here on earth; from Abraham to Moses, the prophets, the disciples, Paul, and you.

The question put to Jesus was more than a question of economics or politics, but a question of conscience. We have that same question today. What should we do when our allegiance to Caesar, or some modern form of Caesar, conflicts with our allegiance to Christ?

Have you noticed in the gospels that Jesus rarely ever lays down specific rules and regulations? He speaks of principles by asking questions. On this day, he asks a very important one.

Maybe this brief story about men trying to entrap Jesus is more than just an interesting anecdote. Maybe it is more than a record of a clever ending. It speaks to us, for sure. How can we say that we are never faced with the dilemma of choosing between Christ and something else we really, really want?

What it finally amounts to is finding that tipping point that upsets a delicate balance. We are citizens of both a heavenly realm and an earthly realm. We must live in both up to a point in which this dual citizenship presents a moral conflict (there's that word again) and then we let God's guidance direct us from that point. In the meantime, we owe a debt to the country we live in for safety from lawless people, for public services we enjoy, for public education, infrastructure of our environment, and the list goes on.

As the Apostle Peter later said, "Fear God. Honor the Emperor." (1 Peter 2:17).

Christians often rage against secularism, the "Fallen World" and "Evil Forces." Whether intentional or not, it can become easy to assume that Christians are engaged in a battle against non-Christians—but we're not.

Failure in citizenship is failure of Christian duty. As Christians, we live and worship in a dimension where heaven and earth overlap. Isn't that what we expect our leaders to recognize in this day and age? And what if that behavior is not forthcoming? We are fortunate to live in a free country where our voices can be heard, where the opportunity exists to show ourselves according to the image of God in which we are made.

What stops us?

As ambassadors of God's image, we are couriers of the truth. Scriptures, when taken in the context of the whole Bible, will bring truth into focus and we can project that image onto the screen of this world. As God's agents, we will not fear seeking the truth from *any* source that points toward and echoes the will and work of our God of the Bible.

I believe that all humankind is searching for God. They may not know that's what they're looking for, but they know something is missing. Look at all the deities various tribes have conjured up. Even in modern society, human nature has not changed. We can be assured that those who know we are Christians are watching us. Do our actions away from Sunday in church support the title of 'Christian'? Or do they make us out to be liars?

There will be trials, entrapments, criticisms, mockery of those who believe. When it happens, you will be in good company. Heavenly company, actually. Stand your ground and fear not. Look toward God and know that he knows your thoughts.

And remember you are not alone in an earthly sense. Lean on each other. Together, you are the body of Christ. Seek reassurance from each other. When your Christian brother or sister seeks you out as a source of strength in time of challenge or sorrow, do not turn them away. Take seriously the image of family, church family, especially in this time in which we face so many challenges to our faith and so much social upheaval.

The message that God loves everyone is radical and controversial and absurd in terms of the world, but according to the Bible, it's true, and as followers of Christ we should boldly show the same love. So, no matter how you feel about your faith, simply ask God to give you the strength and capacity to follow Christ's example! Walk with God. Christianity is not a religion; it's a way of life. Christianity can be messy, grueling, uncomfortable, and requiring an extraordinary amount of time, energy, effort, and grace. But God's voice is soft and gentle and speaks to you in that secret hidden place in your heart.

But even in God's image, to be human is to make mistakes. Christianity doesn't change that. You'll still stumble and make horrible decisions, but the difference is that you'll have the reassurance of God's grace, mercy, and love.

Amidst all the mountains of earthly things that (for now) belong to Caesar, you are what belongs to God. Ask yourself the question, "Who am I and why am I here?" You are the tools by which He will bring His will to this earth. You are an instrument of His peace. What a privilege! What an honor!

I belong to Him
He has work for me to do.
Joy I can't describe!

Questions for Discussion

1. Can you distinguish the boundary that separates earthly citizenship from heavenly citizenship?
2. Do the two overlap?
3. Can the two be in conflict?

Chapter Six
To Love is To Live

Matthew 25:31-46

[31] "When the Son of Man comes in his glory, and all the angels with him, then he will sit on the throne of his glory. [32] All the nations will be gathered before him, and he will separate people one from another as a shepherd separates the sheep from the goats, [33] and he will put the sheep at his right hand and the goats at the left. [34] Then the king will say to those at his right hand, 'Come, you that are blessed by my Father, inherit the kingdom prepared for you from the foundation of the world; [35] for I was hungry and you gave me food, I was thirsty and you gave me something to drink, I was a stranger and you welcomed me, [36] I was naked and you gave me clothing, I was sick and you took care of me, I was in prison and you visited me.' [37] Then the righteous will answer him, 'Lord, when was it that we saw you hungry and gave you food, or thirsty and gave you something to drink? [38] And when was it that we saw you a stranger and welcomed you, or naked and gave you clothing? [39] And when was it that we saw you sick or in prison and visited you?' [40] And the king will answer them, 'Truly I tell you, just as you did it to one of the least of these who are members of my family, you did it to me.' [41] Then he will say to those at his left hand, 'You that are accursed, depart from me into the eternal fire prepared for the

devil and his angels; [42] *for I was hungry and you gave me no food, I was thirsty and you gave me nothing to drink,* [43] *I was a stranger and you did not welcome me, naked and you did not give me clothing, sick and in prison and you did not visit me.'* [44] *Then they also will answer, 'Lord, when was it that we saw you hungry or thirsty or a stranger or naked or sick or in prison, and did not take care of you?'* [45] *Then he will answer them, 'Truly I tell you, just as you did not do it to one of the least of these, you did not do it to me.'* [46] *And these will go away into eternal punishment, but the righteous into eternal life."*

* * * * *

I have often wondered why goats get a bad reputation in scriptures like this one. Have you ever seen a baby goat? If you want to see an example of something cute, go look at a baby goat.

In biblical times, goats were commonly flocked together with sheep. But goat hair is not the same as sheep's wool. Goat hair was tough, rugged, and used for making ropes, tents, carpets, sacks, and slings, among other things. Goat meat was considered clean and was eaten when beef or mutton was not available. They could be used in Hebrew sacrifice.

In Leviticus, God instructs Moses how two goats are to be brought to the priest, one for sacrifice and the other to be the scapegoat. That is, the priest lays his hands on the head of the scapegoat and transfers all the sins of the people onto the goat (Leviticus 16:8-10). The animal is then taken into the wilderness and released, taking the people's sins with him.

They wouldn't think of doing that with a sheep. Sheep were regarded with higher esteem. Their wool was more delicate and used for finer things. They were the preferred animal for sacrifice. Sheep had more value and respect. They represented higher things than did a goat.

Even the sound of the two names gives 'goat' a more vulgar connotation, at least in my opinion. So, there is historical precedence in distinguishing sheep from goats in the manner Jesus describes.

Some will use the excuse that discerning right from wrong is not a simple task. Indeed, there are issues that depend on one's perspective and perspective can vary from person to person.

But Jesus made it simple for us. He said love each other as we love ourselves. There's another way to understand this and it involves what we do at the beginning of each day. We get up each morning, think of our basic needs and take care of them. As you pass by your dresser, you might look in the mirror. Do you care about the person you see? Is that person hungry? Sick? Lonely? Worried? Sad? What will you do about it? If you have an ounce of self-respect, you will think of something. Can you care for others in the same way?

Look at our reading again. Who does he list? It mentions the hungry, the thirsty, the naked, the sick, the incarcerated. In other words, it focuses on the vulnerable, those who have no voice, those who are desperate, those with no family or friends.

It does not mention anyone who might have lost some cash on the stock market that day, or someone whose internet is not working that day. Just having a bad day does not qualify for being listed as someone in need.

So, when do you qualify? Wait until your loses mount up and you have nowhere to turn, no one to comfort you, no one to sit with you and share your pain. When life's events reduce you to the helplessness of a child, that's when you qualify. Even as an adult, you may feel a sense of detachment from the world around you, a sense of being in a foreign place where nobody knows who you are, or cares, for that matter.

And you will hope and pray that someone, somewhere, somehow will have read this passage and will be there for you by the grace of God. You will hope that people will love you the way they love themselves, know your pain, your hunger, your loneliness. Most people will pass you by, like the characters in the Good Samaritan story. Most folks have an excuse.

It occurred to me that I have probably been one of those with an excuse at certain times. My biggest excuse is to say I cannot save every puppy in the dog pound. I really think that is a true statement, but there are times when that excuse is so handy, so readily available that maybe I over-use it.

I am a great follower of lists. I don't know about you, but I get up each morning with a mental list of what my day will be, what things I must accomplish. Most of the things on my list are for me and no one else. Mow the yard, take out the trash, peck away at the computer keyboard; things that I and I alone want or need to do.

My morning prayer, if I remember to put it on my list, should be as Philip Yancey tells us, to ask God to show us what His will is for that day and how we can be part of it.[1] What is God's script for the day and what lines do I have in life's drama?

I'm not one to issue guarantees, but if we ask God that question about His will for us, I can guarantee He will answer somehow, and we need to be listening. And if we are listening, then throughout the day we may see the vulnerable, the helpless, the hopeless among the family of God, if that is what He has in mind for us that day.

Speaking of family, I hope we all have those who love us, family and extended family. I'm sure you do, in one way or another. And I'm sure you love them in return, in one way or another.

That's well and good, but Jesus says it's easy to love someone who loves you. Even the Pharisees can do that, he says.

Why is it so easy to love someone who loves you? When you are loved, how does it make you feel about yourself? I have nothing against family love, God knows I don't! But it does bring into play a bit of that self-love you felt when you looked in the morning mirror. It boosts your self-esteem and, next to God's grace, self-esteem is our most treasured possession! Like many other people, I tend to gravitate toward what makes me feel good about myself.

What about the hungry, the lonely, the sick? What shape is their self-esteem in? A better question is: What can I do about it?

The scripture mentions prisons. Ever been to one? I would say we all have. Not all prisons are places of physical incarceration with bars and locks and guards. What about prisons of the heart, invisible chains that hold us fast and keep us from feeling the beauty and taste of the world around us?

Do we know anyone with painful memories, the kind that each day they must work upon to suppress and keep buried? Do they conceal a guilt, an inadequacy that gnaws at the soul and builds walls to keep others out? If that's not a prison, tell me what it is.

But notice that Jesus is not asking you to do brain surgery or anything wildly complicated. He's not asking you to do anything that any normal human being cannot do. A moment of your time, a cup of cold water, a sandwich from the deli in the market for the hungry man standing outside on the sidewalk, a word of encouragement, maybe just a passing smile, maybe that's enough.

Such small things have a dual effect. The most obvious is what it does to the recipient. But the other effect is what it does to you. Being good to others, even in small bites, can be addictive. It can be uplifting, but only if you are doing it for the other person.

If we are to become addicted to anything, let it be this! There is joy, justifiable joy in being an instrument of God's peace, to be the face of Christ to someone else, to love someone as you love yourself, to love what God loves.

That is how we will be judged. That is what will separate the sheep from the goats.

Just as we have done this for the least of God's family, we have done it for Him. By the same token, what we withhold from the least of these, we withhold from Him.

We might ask, "I have known people who do good things and never darken the door of a church, don't know the first thing about the Bible and couldn't care less about what God says or wants. Yet, they do good things. Can you explain that?"

They do good things.... How do you know? Because you see them doing it? Is that all?

Can we see what's in their heart? Can we see what is the source of their goodness, their motivation? Better yet, can they see it? Do they realize that everything good comes from God? Is it possible that God is working through them? God gave them a heart that beats, lungs that breathe, and a brain that thinks. Do these things stop if a person is not a believer? So, the question is, can God work good through a non-believer? I don't have the answer, so I am hesitant to pass judgement.

Does God use deeds done for others to speak to someone's heart as they are doing it? Have you ever been called by God to do something, something that works for the good of someone else?

How did it make you feel? Did you feel God's will working in you? The next time you see a non-believer doing something good for someone else, look for the chance to tell him or her that you believe it came from God. They will probably deny it, but you've planted a seed of thought. Tell them that they are an instrument of God's peace, and let it go with just that thought. Then step back and trust

God to do His work. The world is set up in such a way that all events, tragic or otherwise, can be bent toward good. The choice toward good is always there; God sees to it.

I would venture to say that doing good for others without feeling the presence of God in Christ makes the whole thing shallow. What an enlightenment such people are missing when they do not realize the very source of their own goodness.

Barclay's commentary, *The Daily Study Bible Series* tells us that three things seem to come out of Matthew 25:

First, it tells us about God. He is involved in our lives, in the stark messiness of our human lives. And it would appear that He loves every minute of it. Perhaps God is like the baker who is creating a lovely loaf of bread, but with hands covered with flour and dough. God is in your neighbor, the one who needs you; especially the weak, the vulnerable, the children. Go ahead, get your hands dirty.

Next, it speaks of a last judgement. What you do in this life will make a difference. Just wondering, how many of us have read the Book of Revelation from start to finish? If you have, you have my utmost admiration and my complete sympathy. There are probably as many interpretations of that book as there are people who have read it. But it is possible that Matthew 25 is really all you need to remember.

This chapter speaks of the future and tells us there will be a day; a day when some people will ask, "What the dickens is going on?"

and others will be dancing and shouting, "I knew it! I knew it! It's really happening!"

On that day, all our lives will be on parade. And we will be judged and separated according to the love we have embraced, the conviction we have exercised between right and wrong, our genuineness as human beings.

This is one of the most vivid parables Jesus ever taught. The lesson is very clear. That is, we will be judged according to our response to human need. God's judgement will not be based on church attendance, contributions to the collection plate, how loud we pray or sing. God does not have a clipboard with tabulations for each of us.

The third thing about this passage is that it is not political, social, economic or anything else like that. It is personal, very personal. God wants not only a world modeled on the values that Jesus taught us; He wants us. He wants our hearts. He wants to save us from obsessing about ourselves and look to those who need us, the least of his family. He wants us to be truly human.

What we need most is to know that God really wants to be intimately close to us. God is not a remote, detached deity that is somewhere out of our reach. In fact, the overarching theme of the whole Bible is God's love for humanity.

We need to feel the touch of God. We need to feel His strength, His light in the darkness, His voice at our shoulder, His calm in our moments of distress. We need to know He is part of our heart. Others need to feel it, as well. You are God's tools on this earth. We are challenged to be the face of Christ to all of God's family. Burn that into your hearts and follow it. Then don't worry about judgement day; don't wonder if God sees you as a sheep or a goat.

Love others as we love ourselves and that covers a lot.

What a daunting task!
We all are the face of Christ.
What a joy to feel!

Questions for Discussion

1. When we ask God to show His will to us, how do we know He's listening?
2. How does God show you the results of your good works? Or does He?
3. Do you have a strong grasp of 'loving yourself' when you are told to love others?

Notes:

1. Philip Yancey, *Prayer,* (Grand Rapids, Zondervan, 2006)

Chapter Seven
You Only Live Twice

Mark 8:31-38

[31] *Then he began to teach them that the Son of Man must undergo great suffering, and be rejected by the elders, the chief priests, and the scribes, and be killed, and after three days rise again.* [32] *He said all this quite openly. And Peter took him aside and began to rebuke him.* [33] *But turning and looking at his disciples, he rebuked Peter and said, "Get behind me, Satan! For you are setting your mind not on divine things but on human things."*

[34] *He called the crowd with his disciples, and said to them, "If any want to become my followers, let them deny themselves and take up their cross and follow me.* [35] *For those who want to save their life will lose it, and those who lose their life for my sake, and for the sake of the gospel, will save it.* [36] *For what will it profit them to gain the whole world and forfeit their life?* [37] *Indeed, what can they give in return for their life?* [38] *Those who are ashamed of me and of my words in this adulterous and sinful generation, of them the Son of Man will also be ashamed when he comes in the glory of his Father with the holy angels."*

****

The eighth chapter of Mark is about halfway through the book and Jesus has shown the disciples, bit by bit, who and what he was. Just by way of rapid review, at this point Jesus has called his first disciples, driven out evil spirits, healed many afflictions, confronted the Pharisees, preached to crowds, given several parables for further understanding, calmed a storm, raised a dead child, fed five thousand, and later fed four thousand, and walked on water.

That's a pretty good resume.

And the disciples, now twelve in number, are starting to have an idea of who they are dealing with. But their idea is not completely the right one. In fact, much of the meaning behind what Jesus did on various occasions went right over their heads.

I always get the feeling as I read the opening verses in chapter one of the Gospel of Mark that the author is in a terrible rush, that he can't wait to reach the place where he feels the Gospel really begins. He says absolutely nothing about how Jesus was born. He gets through the baptism in no time flat. He barely mentions the temptation in the wilderness. And only then, after racing through those first fourteen verses, does he get where he seems to have been racing to—the real beginning as he sees it—and that is the opening words of Jesus himself. Up to that point it has all gone so fast that hardly anybody except John the Baptist knows as yet who Jesus really is, just as it might be said that most of the time hardly any of us know as yet who Jesus really is.

With each passing event, the disciples are more and more convinced that Jesus will be another fire-brand leader like they had known of in the past, ignoring the fact that these previous leaders turned out to be just a flash in the pan with a short shelf-life. But they were sure that Jesus was to be the one who would finally bring freedom from oppression, a conquering king, another King David. But there was just something about Jesus that was different from the others. They simply could not put their finger on it, but there was something special in this man.

Finally, when Jesus asks who they think he is, Peter answers with his famous confession that he, Jesus, is the Christ, the Son of the Living God.

That was Jesus' cue, I guess. Jesus drops a bomb on their thoughts.

He tells them to sit down and listen because he has something to tell them. His news is not about how he is going to resist and conquer, but how he is going to be persecuted and made to suffer by the local rulers who will not believe him and, in fact, will kill him.

That last part probably gave them a jolt that stopped all thoughts of splendor. I wonder how clearly they heard the next part in which he tells them that he will rise up after three days. It would be totally understandable if the disciples still had, running through their heads, the prospect that someone is going to kill Jesus!

Put yourself in their shoes. "Did I hear right? Did he say what I think he said? No, that can't be!"

Someone else who might have been listening more closely says, "Yeah, but did you hear the part about rising up from the dead? In three days – yeah!"

These men have left jobs and family, witnessed some real miraculous things by a wonderful man and now he says this?

How did they get roped into this in the first place? Have you ever been in a position in which you felt like you had painted yourself into a corner and did not know how to get out of it? Multiply that several times and we might have an inkling of how these men felt.

There was probably a feeling of disbelief, maybe even betrayal. This is not what they signed up for. What a way to start a ministry!

I am reminded of a movie scene in which a group of B-17 bombers were flying into Hawaii on the day Pearl Harbor was bombed. They had no ammunition, no way to defend themselves and were low on fuel. They had no choice but to keep on flying.

The commander of the lead aircraft said, "This is one heck of a way to fly into a war!" There was no turning back.

The disciples probably had some version of that same feeling. The dilemma was real, and the stakes had just gotten higher, much higher. They probably felt like an anvil had fallen on them.

All the dreams of the Jewish nation about a new king, one from the line of David, one who would free them from centuries of oppression, came crashing down on their hopes.

Some men take disappointment and bury it, hide their emotions. Not Peter; not good old, hot-headed Peter! He challenges Jesus about the death prediction. We do not know if Peter's response was out of anger or anguish, but we can surmise that it was unmistakably visceral.

Peter's response to Jesus reminds me of a scowling, frowning teacher who rudely corrects a student in front of the whole class for giving the wrong answer to a question. How ironic is it that in previous verses, Peter has just said that Jesus is the Messiah and now he has the audacity to admonish - the Messiah?

So typical of Peter! How many times do we try to put words in God's mouth? How many times do we try to impose our will on God? Here is yet another example of how well-meaning people can still be wrong.

Jesus' response is not toward Peter but toward Satan. Remember it was not that long ago that Jesus dealt with Satan in the wilderness. He tells the group that their thinking is based on earthly logic, not heavenly thinking, the same logic that would believe the Messiah was another David, a John Wayne of the first century.

This brings up a point about Peter that we all have in common with him. There is a side of us, each of us, that is vulnerable to being duped or exploited. Satan comes in only when we give him the key to the back door. But we have the authority to rebuke and eject him when he tries to make us part of his plans. That's what Jesus did in Peter's case. It was more than just rebuking Satan; it was a lesson in how to do it.

Jesus knew his disciples' thoughts. He always does. They were looking for a winning score, a victory lap, a blare of trumpets. They were still looking for a feel-good event.

Jesus tells them the opposite will happen. He tells them that following him will require that they focus away from themselves. He tells them they will have to deny themselves if they want to follow him.

That's strong language. Deny oneself. Does that mean to do without certain pleasures or luxuries? Is it that simple? Actually, it means to place God as the foremost thing in your life and make self a second-place runner. Maybe a close second, but certainly not first.

In fact, self-denial is the first step. One cannot be in God's plan without it. Focus on self has been humanity's root problem since the garden since the beginning of time. The serpent told Eve she could be as good as God, that she could focus on self. Who needs God?

Furthermore, Jesus told his disciples that they must take up their cross and follow. Who said anything about a cross? How did that come into the discussion? Take up my cross? I did not know I had one.

How often have we heard someone say, amid an imposed, unavoidable hardship, that a certain stroke of bad luck was their cross to bear.

We might say, "Life has been unfortunate for him, poor soul, and I guess that's just his cross to bear!"

That is a grossly inaccurate meaning of what Jesus said. To take up one's cross for Jesus does not mean to take up one's bad roll of the dice.

It means take up a cross that you choose to take up. Jesus already knew how he was going to die, so the cross was a central figure in his thoughts and words. And apparently, he had already *chosen* that path for his life. The transfiguration made that clear. He asks us to make a choice. We have already said that Christianity can be messy, and we have a choice about diving into it.

By the same token, he said if we want to save our life, we will lose it, meaning if our primary concerns are for earthly survival, then our days are numbered. But if we choose to live our life for him, with our focus turned away from the things of an earthly life, we will find eternity with him.

This is at the center of Christian life.

Why does such a glorious choice have to be so hard? Fact is, it does not have to be hard. The ways of the world have made it hard. The cross we choose would not be a cross if the world had not made it so. But it is what it is. Wishing won't make it go away.

Bringing the message of Christ by living the example is like carrying the right food into a room of hungry people who do not know what nutrition they need until you explain it to them.

Jesus mentions the comparison between gaining the whole world and yet losing one's life. Perhaps it would be logical to see it as immediate gratification rather than delayed gratification.

I once heard about a fascinating experiment done by child psychologists. A large group of pre-school children were given a choice. They could have a cookie now, or if they would prefer to wait ten minutes, they could have two cookies. Ten minutes to a preschooler can seem like a long time. Some wanted their pleasure now and some opted to wait. Those who waited sat and watched their friends eat their single cookie.

Twenty-five years later, after keeping track of these children as they were growing up, they looked to see what each one had accomplished in their lives. On average, those who had opted for a ten-minute delay in gratification were, on average, in leadership positions and professional careers. Those who chose immediate pleasure generally had less productive lifestyles.

Those who were willing to make sacrifices with the future in mind reaped a bigger reward. It was based on the belief that there was something worth waiting for.

We have all seen the bumper sticker that says, "Drive safely, the life you save may be your own."

We have two lives, if you believe what Jesus says in this chapter's verses. I ask you, which life do we want to save? Do we believe there is actually a choice in the matter?

As you contemplate that choice, the cross changes everything. It asks, what do we value? When our earthly life ends, we become a memory to others. It is over for us, and it will leave others to deal with the reality of it. But the other life, the heavenly life, is still in question. What happens there depends on what had happened here.

Jesus tells these men that if they are ashamed of him now, he will have no choice but to look the other way when they come before the throne to be judged.

Our lives are like money in the pocket. It does no good sitting in that pouch. It only has value when it is spent. The life God gives us is not to keep, but to spend. Oddly, these two lives are, in the beginning, running parallel at the same time. While we exist on this earth, with lungs breathing and hearts beating, we can also be living the life God offers us. He gives us reason to have joy in our lives, the thrill of knowing we are special and loved.

To spend one's life as Jesus would want means to ask certain questions. We put aside questions like, "How much can I get?" and replace it with, "How much can I give?"

We should be asking ourselves what it means for us to be Christians. It should be a call to discipleship. There are no shortcuts. God does not fit into a side shelf on the trophy case where we take Him down whenever we feel like it.

Just as the disciples slowly realized who Jesus was, we should be on the same journey to know who he is, both in this earthly life and the heavenly life which has already begun.

Don't miss that train. You can still hop on.

We all lead two lives.
Two roads running parallel.
One is a dead end.

Questions for Discussion

1. Why would the Jews think the coming Messiah would be a conquering soldier-king?
2. If God has the desire for all of us to be 'saved,' why did Jesus have to die in order to accomplish that? As you form your answer, think of the main theme of the bible, God's love for us.
3. For those who are believers in Christ, has eternal life already started?

Chapter Eight
Shepherds

Somewhere along the pathway to becoming a Commissioned Pastor, you will cross paths with the subject of pastoral care. There will come a time when someone will, when you least expect it, come to you and ask for help. The title of 'Pastor' with any number of qualifying adjectives carries a message that you are capable and available to listen, to care, to comfort. It's part of the job. I came into the commissioning process having had the experience of a series of transforming events that equipped me for the job and gave me a perspective that was like wandering into a foreign country; foreign but, in a way, so familiar. Most of us have the tools needed to be caregivers to those who have gone through a life-changing loss of some type. We just don't know how to use them.

God introduced me to this thought process in a painful way.

It was February 18, 1997, when I lost my dream job. It was on a Tuesday around 2 PM when my boss called me into his office and my eyes locked on the Division Director and our Human Resources representative, both sitting at a small conference table with anxious looks on their faces.

Before that day, I paid no attention to the small footnote in the church bulletin which said, "If you are going through hard times or have suffered a life changing loss, Stephen Ministers are here to help you." The following Sunday, that little footnote jumped off the page and surrounded me like a thousand voices. I now look back on that time as a life changer. Stephen Ministry had launched me on an eye-opening journey of immense Christian growth. Allow me to tell you about it.

Emotional wounds hurt as much as physical wounds. Both types will heal, but without the attention of a competent caregiver, healing is slow, and scars run deep.

Understanding self-esteem is at the root of it all. You have read on previous pages that next to God's grace, self-esteem is the most important treasure we have. When we feel positive about ourselves, we are happy, productive, and clear thinking. But esteem is like fine, delicate crystal that shatters when struck the wrong way and we learn to unconsciously protect it. So, most people create a surrounding layer of emotional insulation which serves as an instinctive mechanism to get them through the potholes in life, but sometimes there's a gap in that protection and the inner self takes a hit. In so many ways, self-esteem is potentially wounded any time there is a sense of loss. There is a minute sense of loss even when you can't find your car keys, but it takes only a nanosecond to recover. How quickly do we get over the big losses like loss of a loved one, loss of a marriage, loss of a job? We may silently ask ourselves, "Did I love that person enough before she died? Was I fair in our relationship? Should I have done something differently?" Too late now. If we are not sinking in self-judgment, we may find ourselves immersed in total chaos and confusion as our jumbled thoughts make no sense. We ask, "Why can't my feelings return to normal? I thought I was tougher than this." God knows, I've had those thoughts.

We have all heard about the value of talking to a friend. Yes, good advice, but pick your friends carefully. We all live in a fix-it world. Our society lives at a fast pace and many people who want to help often offer the wrong kind of help. We all focus on results because we were taught to do so. It's how we go from day to day. But for those trying to extract themselves from the pit of grief, struggling to just get through the day, are swallowed by depression and sorrow. They don't need a "fix-it", they need a process. It's good and kind for others to make material fixes for you, but when the last well-wisher has gone home, it's still just you and your tangled web of thoughts. Nothing will have changed. Oddly, family members can sometimes be the worst of the "fix-it" folks.

The need is for someone who listens effectively and focuses on the process. Someone who will confidentially listen to your most personal thoughts without judging you. Someone who will give you unconditional positive regard, share your tears and assure you that your feelings are valid.

Another way to look at it: to focus on results means outcomes that are in the future. By contrast, the process entails things I can do now, today, for someone else. So, we must make a distinction between caregiver vs cure-giver. This frees us up from any fear of failure and gives the care receiver his or her own sense of self-accomplishment.

Is that dodging responsibility? Not really. It puts things in their proper place. We are the caregiver and God is the cure-giver.

Good listeners are hard to find. Pastors are usually regarded as good listeners. They extinguish the flames like firefighters and would like to stick around to help with the re-building process, but they can't because there's another fire somewhere else. Stephen Ministers are extensions of their pastor, and they can stay for the long haul. They are not professional counselors, psychologists, or therapists. Rather, they are caring Christians who want to help in the best way possible and have received many hours of training in topics such as the art of listening, understanding human emotions, the mechanics of human crisis, confidentiality, recognizing signs of depression or potential suicide, and above all else: knowing their limitations. Stephen Ministers do not attempt anything that should be reserved for professionals.

Effective caregiving is a team effort. Stephen Ministers do not operate in a vacuum. They meet twice each month in peer supervisory sessions and, in total confidentiality, discuss the relationships they have with their care receivers. Names are never mentioned in these meetings. Care receivers should feel safe and private when talking to a Stephen Minister.

Stephen Ministry is a total program designed to recruit, organize, train, and support lay ministers who give confidential one-on-one pastoral-type care to those who have gone through losses of any kind and need emotional and spiritual healing.

Stephen Ministers and Commissioned Pastors make a good team. Even better if they are one in the same person.

Stephen Ministry was created in 1975 by Dr. Kenneth Haugk, a Lutheran pastor in St. Louis. Forty-eight years later, there are Stephen Ministers in all 50 states, 32 different countries, and over 190 different Christian denominations. To date, over 75,000 Stephen Leaders have been trained as well as over 600,000 Stephen Ministers. This ministry is found in over 12,000 churches worldwide and the number is growing.

Stephen Ministers will gladly tell how they receive a deeply fulfilling, healthy combination of God-pleasing self-esteem and humility because we know we have answered a calling and feel like a useful part of the body of Christ. Over time, the experience of caring for someone in a distinctive way will take you far down your Christian pathway and you will see more of the whole context of God's mission in the world. Your priorities and your vision will change. Your relationship to God will become more intimate. Mine certainly did.

For most, there is always the issue of finding time for this ministry. God always has a way of providing the time. If you love what you're doing, the question of time is usually a moot point. I assure you; Stephen Ministry is like a good book you can't put down.

Have you ever crossed paths with someone who just lost a loved one and you just didn't know what to say? Stephen Ministry will teach you what to say.

Some may think Stephen Ministers should be expert theologians. Make no mistake, this is a caring ministry. People in pain need love and caring, not theology or dogma.

In Matthew 25, Christ said, "When you do this to the least of my brethren, you do it to me." It tells us when you give of your time, when you listen, really listen to someone else's grief, when you validate the feelings of someone who feels alone in a cruel world, when you help someone heal from the wounds of loss and fear, you do it for Him.

Do you leave church each Sunday with the feeling that you are not fulfilling your life's purpose in God's plan? Stephen Ministry is looking for those who want to help on a personal level. You will learn that God does indeed operate on our level, not in some mystical, puzzling context that we are not supposed to understand. The tools of Stephen Ministry make sense.[1,2]

In 2005, while a member of United Presbyterian Church of Whitinsville in Massachusetts, I took on the task of organizing a Stephen Ministry group. First, I traveled to Pittsburgh for an intense one-week conference about Stephen Ministry Leadership. Then I came home and began to recruit groups of fellow church members to be trained as Stephen Ministers at the local level. Stephen Ministry headquarters in St. Louis provides all the material you need for this level of training. It involves 18 topics and approximately 50 hours of training time. It can be accomplished in 4-5 months. In Whitinsville, we trained three groups over several years. Even though the interactions between caregiver and care receiver are confidential, the rest of the congregation knows it's there and it makes a difference in the spiritual awareness of the members.

From Massachusetts, I moved to Kissimmee, Florida where I had lived once before and, conveniently, had a church home to come back to. Dr. Frank Allen was the pastor when I left, and he was still there when I returned. I told him I was looking for a church home where I could do the same thing as we did in Massachusetts; that is, start a Stephen Ministry group. He looked at me and just blinked and swallowed hard.

As it turns out, Dr. Allen had just returned from a Saturday workshop directed by Stephen Ministry, and he was impressed with the presentation. So impressed was he that the Session of his church gave him a green light to proceed with enrolling his congregation if he could find someone to spearhead the project.

And there we sat on a back pew of an empty sanctuary, just before lunch on a Sunday, both feeling God's presence and having no doubt what He was telling us to do. Stephen Ministry at First Presbyterian Church of Kissimmee, Florida was a success and went on to provide care for a significant number of people. I have since moved to Virginia and the church I left in Florida continues that ministry.

Pastoral Care was one of the topics covered in the program I was enrolled in with The University of Dubuque Theological Seminary in preparation for pastoral commissioning in December of 2016. The didactic material of that course was like reuniting with an old friend because of my experience in Stephen Ministry.

It would be difficult, if not impossible, to give you all the details of human distress encountered as a Stephen Minister in the span of one chapter. But there are some major highlights that can give you a perfunctory sampling of the extent and depth of it.

Many people avoid talking about feelings because they equate feelings with weakness. Better stated, people feel vulnerable when they open up and talk about feelings and emotions.

That applies especially to the men in our society. General Norman Schwarzkopf had an interview with Barbara Walters in which she asked him about his sons and the General became somewhat teary-eyed. His masculinity was not so fragile that it could be bruised by a simple show of emotion. I assure you the work is not some touchy-feely over-dramatized program.

Love and communication are the lifeblood of human lives and emotion is the language of these things. Feelings and emotions are the 'stuff' that make human lives, well, human.

Fear of showing emotion is the one big hurdle that blocks care receivers from asking for help. It takes courage to ask for help, and it reflects the human vulnerability we all have (another example of human conflict). Feelings and emotions are, unmistakably, a human thing. We are wired that way. The history of the world is written with the ink of human emotions.

To understand the feelings of others starts with understanding of our own feelings. Every psychologist will agree with me on that. In our training, we shared life experiences with each other as a means of reminding us how hard it is for others to open their hearts and say what they are feeling.

We learn about ourselves in this process. We cannot deal with the emotions of others unless we can deal with our own. We often see ourselves in others. So, we must cope with our own emotions before we can be of help to anyone else.

Some emotions are very small, almost unnoticed. Vincent Van Gogh said, "Let's not forget that the little emotions are the great captains of our lives, and we obey them without realizing it."

Our thoughts can be transferred to body language and then noticed by a listener. People in pain are more perceptive of tone of voice and body language, so we must learn to keep our thoughts on track. They are often times expecting you to judge them as being weak and unable to handle their own issues, even if you tell them that you are not judging them!

That brings us to our next subject, a major tool in pastoral care: listening.

In every encounter between Jesus and someone he had just met, the first thing he did was listen. Any kind of communication between people is precious and holy.

Most people think they know how to listen when, in fact, they are just waiting for their turn to talk, which means inattention to the silent signals from the victim. Father Henri Nouwen told the story of his own experience in trying to minister to hurricane victims. He saw a woman sitting on the front steps of what used to be her home. With every good intention, he sat next to her and gave her every reason he could think of to be positive and hopeful. When he left, it was obvious she felt worse than before he had arrived. He had tried to cheer up a victim at a time when it was more appropriate to be sad. He then realized he hadn't been listening.

The care receiver must feel safe. Create a safe place. Pastoral Care ministry is confidential. Care receivers should be able to talk to us with the utmost trust. Picture the most important person in your younger years. The person who made the room light up when he or she walked into that room. Someone you could trust with your deepest thoughts. Someone you felt safe with. That's how your care receiver should feel about you. It won't happen on the first visit. We all have a secret place where we keep our innermost thoughts. When someone opens his or her thoughts to you, you have been invited as a guest into a very holy place. As a guest, you don't go in and begin to rearrange the furniture.

Henri Nouwen once said, "Listening is an act of love. But if I look closely at this experience of being loved, I notice my greatest joy in being loved is the way it makes me feel about myself. It sends me a clear, unmistakable message that I am good and beautiful and noble. And that is the joy that touches me most deeply!" Take it to the bank; it has to do with self-esteem.

Although we listen, we are not completely silent. However, you should be doing no more than 10% of the talking. Your listening should include gentle inquiry which demonstrates that you understand what you're hearing. You are also striving to keep the conversation alive. The care receiver sets the pace, so you let that person show you where the conversation is going. Your part in the conversation also looks for permission to broach the subject on the scariest, embarrassing, painful things the receiver is going through. As you let them set the pace, their trust in you increases.

When your inquiry poses a crucial question, that is your time to be silent. That's when the care receiver has your blessing to tell you everything; but you'll rarely get *everything*. There's always more to the story. Hopefully, there will be other visits.

When you ask a leading question, there's a couple of hints you might benefit from. The word 'You' at the beginning of a sentence is often seen as accusatory, especially in the mind of someone in pain. There's always at least a crumb of guilt floating in their thoughts. Think about that. Also, the word 'Why' at the beginning of a question can be seen as judgmental. That puts the other person in a defensive mode. Can you explain that? We must think of a better way to ask 'why?' Another way to keep the conversation going is to simply say, "Tell me more."

Stephen Ministry is distinctively Christian Care. Attitude and behavior speak volumes about your Christian foundation without having to vocalize it. You must sincerely believe why you are doing this.

Our goal is to love as Jesus loved, to serve rather than be served. Our servant's towel must be bigger than our ego. Do not ever get the notion that you are just playing with the feelings and thoughts of others. We are not manipulating people into feeling different. What we do is powerful because it is God's will. We are caring for His flock, as He told us to do.

Your servanthood comes with humble, but powerful authority. Have no doubt. God is with you when you give care. We are not Bible-thumpers. We are not trying to impress anyone nor are we trying to recruit church members. I knew of a care receiver who did not want a spiritual guide. She did not want any hint of spirituality. But she knew where it came from. However, the relationship with her Stephen Minister planted a seed that grew. What if we had forced our religious beliefs on her? She would have bolted. What is the nutritional value of uneaten food?

When Jesus confronted the woman accused of adultery, he didn't quote scripture or preach a sermon. He just planted a seed of thought. How many seeds of thought have been planted in your minds? Remember I mentioned those small emotions that are the great captains of our lives? Are they not seeds of thought?

I don't need to tell you, rest assured, God will be with you in this ministry, whether it be as a Stephen Minister or a Commissioned Pastor or both. Joshua was very timid when God told him it was time to cross the Jordan and take the promised land. In Joshua 1:9, God says to Joshua: *Have I not commanded you? Be strong and courageous. Do not be terrified; do not be discouraged, for the Lord your God will be with you wherever you go.* This verse from the story of Joshua tells me that God will not call me (or you) to do anything without giving us the means and the strength to do it. This is not a prosperity verse. It's not about something you dreamed up; it's God's plan and He keeps his word.

We operate with the assumption that most folks have the answers to their struggles but can't clarify reality because their thoughts are in a jumble, and they don't think very highly of themselves because of that.

That's why self-esteem is so important. Although this does not sound like therapy, it can be of great help to some people by helping them focus on the process, not the cure.

We read that God came to earth as Jesus to reconcile humans. Nice words, but if words are all you have, they grow faint with time. We need reminders of God's actions. Stephen Ministry (indeed, all pastoral care) finds its supreme model in Jesus' life and teachings. It doesn't just remind us of him, it gives us the wonderful opportunity to live like he lived; to immerse ourselves in his words rather than just read them like a billboard. It takes time, but all good things take time.

I am very fortunate to have had a prolonged Stephen Ministry experience *before* I started down the path toward being a Commissioned Pastor. But it's not too late. One is not a prerequisite for the other.

It's discipleship and the building of it never stops.

<blockquote>
Make me a watchman.
So many souls are in pain.
Give me warm, skilled hands.
</blockquote>

Questions for Discussion

1. Does self-confidence put you in better touch with God?
2. Why is it hard for people in pain to ask for help?
3. If it is God's will that you help someone, why should we avoid simply stepping in and fixing the problem?

Notes:

1. James E. Sullivan, *The Good Listener,* (Notre Dame, Indiana, Ave Maria Press, 2000)
2. Kenneth Haugk, *Don't Sing Songs To A Heavy Heart,* (St. Louis, Stephen Ministries, 2004)

Chapter Nine

By Their Fruits
(And something about airports)

Matthew 5:13-16

[13] *"You are the salt of the earth; but if salt has lost its taste, how can its saltiness be restored? It is no longer good for anything, but is thrown out and trampled under foot.* [14] *"You are the light of the world. A city built on a hill cannot be hid.* [15] *No one after lighting a lamp puts it under the bushel basket, but on the lampstand, and it gives light to all in the house.* [16] *In the same way, let your light shine before others, so that they may see your good works and give glory to your Father in heaven.*

* * * * *

Several years ago, I was seated on a plane going somewhere and a middle-aged man came to sit beside me. He had that Hollywood look about him with the manicured haircut and a ring and watch that both looked like they came from the same chunk of gold. He said nothing for 15 minutes or so, then turned to me abruptly and asked, "Tell me, young man, are you saved? Do you know Jesus Christ as your Lord and Savior?" All I could do was answer, "Uh, yeah." I then decided to look out the window. I usually look forward to any discussion about God and God's plan, but this guy really turned me off. Nevertheless, and to the credit of the man on the plane, can you imagine how the early apostles were received when they told total strangers that a crucified Jew rose from the dead and is Lord of the world? For many folks, it's hard to believe even today.

I had another airplane experience that still amazes me. A young man sat next to me on a flight from here to there, about a one-hour trip and I noticed a certain air of distress on his face that was noticeable even out of the corner of my eye. My family takes entertainment from remembering situations I have created because of my propensity to talk to total strangers. It has led me to have regrets sometimes, but I have found that people want to talk more than one might imagine, as long as the conversation is not uncomfortable. I guess this young man was looking for someone to talk to because I had barely introduced myself when he started pouring his soul out to me. I must stop here and tell you that he drove the conversation. He asked me if I had children and I said I did, then he asked how they had turned out as teenagers. I told him Jane and I were proud of our boys, and I guess he thought we had some sort of gift for raising kids. I was about to tell him my wife had more talent in that department, but he suddenly told me in a flurry of words like a waterfall that he had a pre-school age daughter, and she apparently had an artistic gift that surpassed many adults. He didn't know what his role was as a father and said his wife was too passive to worry much about it. He was worried about not being a good enough father.

I listened for several minutes, amazed that this young man was avidly spilling out such personal information after having met me only ten minutes before. When he finally paused to take a breath, I assured him that the child would show him what direction she wanted to go and at such a young age, there was plenty of time to watch and love and marvel at the way she was growing up. He looked at me with such a look of relief and it occurred to me that maybe he needed something more.

"Have you talked to God about this?" I asked. He said he didn't know how. I noticed he didn't retreat from the subject, so we had a heart-felt discussion about God's blessings and about prayer.

I had never before had an experience quite like this and I have not had one similar to it since then. It was the right time and the right place and God guided me in the tone and texture of what I said to him. It had not happened because of any expertise on my part; I know God was with us on that plane. His daughter is probably a grown woman now. I wonder how everything turned out.

I recently read a wonderful article in *Christian Century* entitled "Reclaiming the *E* Word," by Debie Thomas (Feb, 2023). She asks why, with all the positive attributes that churches have, are we afraid to invite and practice *evangelism*. She says that even with the passage of time and despite human folly, God's Good News remains good. So, what is our problem?

Spreading the good news of the gospel should be the business of all Christians. We cannot all be preachers, or Sunday school teachers, or missionaries. In fact, preachers cannot always preach every waking moment. How then, are we to spread the good word? I see it as a two-step process. First, the opportunity must present itself and initially all you can do is be on the lookout for it. This is like the hardest part in writing a story; it's like the first sentence on a blank sheet of paper. Where do you begin? Sometimes God digs you in the ribs like my encounter with the young man on the plane.

In John 10:14, Jesus said, "My sheep will know me." That statement is much broader than you think. How many times have you been shopping with someone who says, "I'm not sure what I'm looking for, but I'll know it when I see it." Other times, one may know exactly what the object of the search is. Both extremes fit Jesus' statement. There are folks out there who want to know Jesus, but just haven't met him yet. In fact, they don't know what they're looking for, but they will know when they see him.

The second part is where you come in. Do everyone a favor and try not to ambush anyone. It can be very counterproductive. When you are introduced to someone, you will have a more complete experience if the person doing the introduction is someone you already know. If a total stranger came up to you and said, "I want to introduce you to someone," I think your internal alarms would immediately sound off. You might be thinking, *who is this guy? Why does he want me to meet someone? What's the scam?* The same thing applies when someone is introduced to Jesus for the first time. The person you are with must feel comfortable in your presence as you take on the role of reflecting God. There must be trust and the overall sense that you can guide them as their questions point to small gaps of emptiness in their life; they must feel safe with you and the answers you give.

I doubt there is hardly anyone who hasn't at least heard the name of Jesus. They may not know much about Him, but I'll bet most have heard the name. How do you make the introduction? In a word, do it carefully. Remember, Jesus said his sheep will know him. There are folks who are looking for something, but not sure what it is. They are unknowingly looking for Jesus. Now for a bold statement: I would assume that most of the people who are unknowingly looking for Jesus are not in church on any given Sunday. If they were in church, chances are that they would be much closer to knowing what they are looking for. But we have often said that our job as Christians is not confined to the four church walls on Sunday mornings. That puts us out there in the world, carrying a message. How do you carry it? How do you get it across?

The first thing, in my opinion and as I said in the previous chapter, is to stay in the process and let God handle the results. It's that simple and yet that complicated. Back to the Debie Thomas article: do as Jesus did; he asked questions, told stories, and he listened - really listened. Don't ambush, don't rush the process, and don't worry if you are not around to see the result.

We should make ourselves to be that city on a hill, the candle in a dark room. Our fruits will make us known. Those who are seeking, whether they know it or not, will notice. In the letter to the Galatians, Paul lists examples of these fruits. They are love, joy, peace, patience, kindness, goodness, fidelity, gentleness, and self-control. He goes on to say there is no law against things like that. Again, things *like* that. This last statement implies that his list is not complete, but just examples. Notice he did not list fine words as one of the fruits. Words cannot replace deeds. Big words and elaborate speeches may sound impressive, but beneath the surface they only call attention to the one speaking and not to the one spoken about. Worldly joy is not the same as biblical joy. Worldly joy is a new car, a winning lottery ticket, a refund from the IRS, applause from an audience of listeners.

The joy God gives us is more like a sense of belonging and being loved. Have you ever heard that children who have clearly defined boundaries from their parents are actually happier than children who are allowed to simply run wild with no restriction? The significance lies not in the actual boundaries but in knowing they are loved and that someone thinks they are important. Joy lives inside those boundaries and uncertainty lives outside of them. Outside that boundary of love, we step into the secular world and leave God behind on a closet shelf.

My previous job required some travel, so I was not unfamiliar with airports. I was once waiting on a flight in the Dallas airport when the agent at the gate called for all 'First class and Platinum Club Members' to board first. Others should wait for their zone to be called. Under my breath, I mumbled, "This is what's it's like to be a second-class citizen." A woman standing next to me, also waiting to board, apparently heard what I had said. She turned to me and remarked, "Well, I'm not second-class!" I immediately thought she must be a real joy to live with. But she continued her sentence, "Not in God's eyes, at least." She wasn't trying to engage me in a conversation about salvation, but I could tell she had not left God at home on a bookshelf. There was no joy in waiting for her flight, but abundant joy in knowing that she was within God's flock.

So be prepared to answer the question as to why you bear such fruit. I have no magic formula for this. Perhaps this part of the chapter should be entitled, 'Mistakes I have made.' This is where your maturity as a Christian comes into play. When someone asks about the source of your good fruits, remember the person asking is someone who has opened himself up to you and is probably just starting a journey of faith. Therefore, a little consideration is needed about human nature. Jesus tells his disciples in Matt 10:16 to be as shrewd as snakes and innocent as doves. The snake in this passage signifies wisdom and timeliness. A snake moves quietly without thrashing about trying to impress anyone. He knows exactly when and how to act. A dove signifies innocence of a child. The dove symbol means that you do no harm in your efforts. You are not asked to become a gushing fountain of pious answers and scriptures. The person making the inquiry of you is probably someone who is venturing onto uncharted territory, so move carefully until you see where the conversation is going.

I think the biggest mistake we make at times like these is that we may become centered on our own words, our own convictions. In doing so, we shift our focus away from the other person's question and call attention to our own self-righteousness. Let the other person set the pace. Ask what they believe and then affirm their thoughts.

Find out what doubts or uncertainties they have. Proceed gently. You are not a spiritual plumber called upon to ream out the clogged conduits of the truth. In the conversation, find those spiritual conduits that are open and focus on them. Find the channels that are working and use them to communicate God's love. Take small steps at first and keep it simple. A person doesn't sit down to a piano for the first time and play Beethoven. You don't land in Madrid and immediately know how to speak Spanish.

So, speaking of the fruits of the Spirit that others can see, let's talk a minute about your own journey. Is your Christian walk a free-flowing stream? If it is, you're in the minority. Lawyers, clergy, those of the healing arts, all such highly trained folks must stop periodically and re-evaluate themselves. As a Christian, you must know where you stand in your journey before you can help others onto that path. What obstacles do you have, what blockages along the way? Christians especially are in need of forgiveness for allowing obstacles to prevent them from being God's ambassadors. Things such as jealousy, unwillingness to forgive, vain pride, gaps in your faith that remain unattended; all are obstacles that Christians may experience. Work on them.

Carrying God's word to others, by any method, requires that you hear and believe with all your heart that God loves you and cares for you. The Apostle Paul said we should pray continuously. I interpret that to mean that God is reflected in everything we say and do. That reflection is part of the process I mentioned earlier. If you are engaged in the process, God is an active partner. When called upon, do you know what to say, how to say it, what not to say? What details of the Christian story do you know? How complete and well-rounded are your Christian disciplines? For example, what good is a tennis player with strong legs, but with weak heart and lungs?

Your ability to become part of the process depends on your Christian virtues and these strengths require work to develop. It is like masterful artwork. It doesn't just happen but requires directed effort. This may serve as a source of discouragement. You may think, "I'm just not able to explain God and Jesus to someone else." Remember this: one foundational principle that predominates in your Christian life is the fact that everything which has come to you as a blessing in this life and the life to come is a gift, not something that you earned. God's love is unconditional. It is the starting point that we Christians all share. Don't be afraid to tell people about it. And don't be ashamed to say you're still in the process of understanding it. Believe this in your heart and say it to those who ask where your faith comes from. It is an ultimate truth. It will project a redemptive image for those who are seeking but not sure what they are looking for.

Let me suggest another way of thinking about it. I don't mean to imply that our fruits can be displayed like a painting you have created through a 'paint by the numbers' kit. It's not about connecting the dots or solving a moral jigsaw puzzle. The first thing to remember is that it's not necessarily about you – your happiness, your fulfillment, your realization. It's about God and God's Kingdom in a genuine human existence similar to the way God displayed it through Jesus.

It's about focusing away from yourself, resisting urges to be center stage. God and God's Kingdom are center stage. This shifts away from the idea that Christian behavior is all about 'keeping the rules' and doing good works. It shifts toward the idea that doing those things which brings God's wisdom and glory into the world will automatically keep the rules and bring about good works. Christian virtue is about the whole of life, not just moral values. And Christian virtue is visible. It makes you stand out in a crowd. You will be that candle in the dark room without intentionally calling attention to yourself. People will notice and wonder how and why you are this way. Make no mistake, you and the one who notices your fruits, are both pilgrims on a journey. So, as you bear witness to God's glory, be ready to learn in the process. Share in the journey.

So, press on with confidence in the Spirit of God and that Spirit will show itself in you. Know the joy that comes from seeing someone else begin their journey and start to experience the ultimate truth of God's love.

I am like a tree.
Good or bad, my fruit is there.
Faith will feed my roots.

Questions for Discussion

1. Why are so many people reluctant to talk about spiritual life?
2. How do you speak about the fruits of your Christian life without seeming to immerse in your own self-praise?
3. How would you speak to someone who feels unworthy of God's love?

Chapter Ten
Smell The Coffee

Sometimes, God's word is revealed slowly, in layers, because we must comprehend at least a glimmer of each layer before we go on to the next. It's like a fine meal at Commander's Palace in New Orleans. That is, one course at a time with something in between each one to clear the palate. In our fast-paced world, most of need to learn to slow down and appreciate the layers.

John 1:1-18

1 *In the beginning was the Word, and the Word was with God, and the Word was God.* *He was in the beginning with God.* *All things came into being through him, and without him not one thing came into being. What has come into being* *in him was life, and the life was the light of all people.*

The light shines in the darkness, and the darkness did not overcome it. There was a man sent from God, whose name was John. He came as a witness to testify to the light, so that all might believe through him. He himself was not the light, but he came to testify to the light. The true light, which enlightens everyone, was coming into the world. He was in the world, and the world came into being through him; yet the world did not know him. He came to what was his own, and his own people did not accept him. [12]But to all who received him, who believed in his name, he gave power to become children of God, [13]who were born, not of blood or of the will of the flesh or of the will of man, but of God. [14]And the Word became flesh and lived among us, and we have seen his glory, the glory as of a father's only son, full of grace and truth.

[15](John testified to him and cried out, "This was he of whom I said, 'He who comes after me ranks ahead of me because he was before me.'") [16]From his fullness we have all received, grace upon grace. [17]The law indeed was given through Moses; grace and truth came through Jesus Christ. [18]No one has ever seen God. It is God the only Son, who is close to the Father's heart, who has made him known.

*****

This chapter is, for the most part, a sermon I gave on January 3, 2021, at First Presbyterian Church of Kissimmee, Florida.

We were at the beginning of a New Year. So often we see the New Year depicted as a baby in diapers, as a new life, a new time, a new awakening. That's how John starts his gospel, from the beginning.

Have you ever wondered what a newborn baby sees when she first opens her eyes? When the first light penetrates through the cornea, passes through the pupil and the fluids, and focuses on the retina? I would imagine it is like seeing creation for the first time.

Have you ever watched a baby when she first discovers her hands? Her eyes dart around from the wrist to the fingertips, and she turns her palms this way and that in amazement like an ancient explorer who has discovered a lost treasure. Does she understand that these digits, these fingernails, these tiny knuckles, belong to her?

Our scripture today is much like that. John's scripture outlines an unfolding process of the good news message. Let's see how it progresses.

John starts us off today at the beginning when humanity first sees the light of day. Something was already there, something big and powerful beyond imagination was there in the form of three facets, three dimensions, three realities.

Humanity did not see what was there, in spite of all the evidence pointing toward it. Maybe, just maybe, early humanity could not comprehend what the light was illuminating. I don't know, but it seems to be a strong possibility.

Eventually, humanity did have the ability to comprehend and that is how John used the metaphor of light.

We have five senses, but vision seems to be the most powerful, both functionally and poetically. If we cannot taste or smell or feel or even hear, we can still manage to exist somewhat. But take away our vision and we are encumbered immensely compared to the loss of the other senses.

Loss of sight is a major adjustment. That is why light versus darkness is one of the most vivid contrasts in our lives.

Not only is light essential for our vision, but light is also energy, light is life. Anyone with even a crumb of knowledge about biology knows that without light, the world would wither and die.

This is not the light John speaks of, but the absence of light in the context of John's opening verses has the same effect. Humanity would wither and cease to be human without the light John speaks of.

Notice that John says when the true light came into the world, the world did not know him. But the true light did not fade away after it appeared.

This light, this true light, does not fit the usual definition of kilowatts or foot-candles. It is the light that shines on our souls, the connection to our Creator and to each other which makes us human.

After creation, it soon became evident that we, in our God-given freedom did not become what God intended. Or maybe we did. We became beings with a choice and the light John speaks of makes clear the path we should be talking to make that choice.

It is a choice that we do not make just once, but every day. And each day that we stay on that right path, the right choice, we step closer and closer to God and become more and more truly human.

John the Baptist knew of this light. His understanding with God was so strong that he knew what was coming. He knew God had a plan. I often wonder where John got his information, his inspiration. We remember that John came from a priestly family. During our Christmas season we talked about what Mary may have understood. Is it mere coincidence that Luke wrote of Mary's experience alongside the similar experience of Elizabeth, John's mother?

From Luke 1:39-40, we know that Mary decided to go visit her cousin, Elizabeth, while both women were carrying their unborn sons. Both women knew their sons would be special and Luke tells us that they shared their special joy with each other. Do you ever wonder what they talked about? How late did they stay up talking that first night?

Further still, when John was born and began to grow, I wonder what Elizabeth told him about his special cousin, this young man named Jesus.

Could we dare to assume that Elizabeth and Zechariah raised their son to know the Old Testament prophecies inside out, backwards and forwards? Of course, we can assume that. Priesthood in those days was passed down through family lines and old Zechariah would have been no different.

Yes, there can be no doubt that John knew what was coming long before it happened. What a blessing it would be if each one of us could have only a fraction of the knowledge and wisdom John possessed.

But it's not like that knowledge was or is hidden from us. It's there. The prophets of the Old Testament still speak to us. If the world had listened, it would have known what John knew: that God would come to us in human form, at the right time, the right place.

What a tragedy, what an irony, that God, through His Word, made the world and yet the world knew Him not. Sounds like today, doesn't it? Things haven't changed much.

In the beginning, we were helpless because we were not only ignorant, but we did not know what we did not know. We did not know what we needed to know.

The effort to show us what we should know comes from God. Funny how in our relationship with God, He always takes the first step.

People around us, in our society, don't seem to know that there is a spiritual wholeness offered to us. They don't see the need.

God doesn't seem relevant.

I think all the things that stand in the way of seeing God as relevant have been formed by humankind. The world is in constant violation of the first commandment which tells us we are to have no other gods before Him. That refers to man-made gods, all of them; some visible, some ideological, some just excuses.

One doesn't have to be a genius to know that today's church attendance and membership is declining. I don't think anyone can say when it actually began, but it was sometime in the late sixties or early seventies.

This should concern us greatly for two reasons: First, any society which does not recognize that purpose in life comes from God will find substitute allegiances. It is no secret that the general view of God among believers is divided into denominations, but all of them have the common denominator of grace from God. These substitute allegiances, however, will have no common denominator except a focus on self. Original sin was just that: focus on self to the exclusion of God.

Secondly, we who believe are looking for more than just a common thread that binds us; we look for salvation because we believe there is a need for it. We believe there is a supreme being we call the Creator who sent His Word to live as flesh among us, carrying and embodying the message of the Good News.

What can we do? In our fast-moving world, the tendency is to say, "Find out why and fix it!"

So easy to say until someone asks where to start. It's not a matter of preaching better sermons or ordering new hymn books. It's not a matter of choosing between traditional service versus contemporary or deciding whether we should paint the interior of the church a different color.

In the early Christian church, folks met wherever and whenever they could because of something they felt, something they believed, not because of so many of the reasons we hear today. They felt a strong tug at their hearts, something they couldn't explain but could only know and feel. It was a matter of relevance.

As a society, that's what we have lost: relevance. God just doesn't seem to matter anymore. How do we correct that?

So much wrong has been done in the name of Christianity down through the centuries and I think it still happens today in other forms. Our attempts to simply make neighborhoods aware of our worship services has met with strong pushback from many directions. Genuine Christian outreach must be done carefully and with depth of thought. The general public is diverse, not only in ethnicity, but in opinions and prior experience. Christian outreach, if done wrong, can be as annoying as robocalls on your phone.

From Philip Yancey, I recently read that the belief in prayer and the frequency of prayer is much stronger in so-called Third World countries than in developed countries.[1] As underdeveloped countries arrive in the 21st century, will they lose their trust in God? Will they follow the pattern of Europe and of this country? Does advancement in technology and science displace God? Does God become an optional feature?

We are so caught up in our own world, we think we can make a designer God to suit our own needs. Sure, I want the model with Bluetooth connections, extended batteries, room to seat six, spoiler on the back, chrome trim, and yes, the God option...the one with a satisfaction guarantee if I decide I don't need it!

I thought it was just a wild exception when I first heard someone say, "I have my own private church, one that God and I agreed on. I don't need to connect with others to be in God's presence, because I have my own private line." And then I began to hear others say basically the same thing, over and over again.

Which tells me this: people still are willing to accept the fact that there is a God but are too lazy to really get to know him. Or maybe not. Maybe it's our fault. Is it possible that God is being portrayed to the public in the wrong way, as if He were a God who was not deeply invested in all the rest of His people, but only in people like me and my own private salvation? There are some highly visible modern-day prophets (?) that speak of God while secretly serving their own agenda. Prosperity preachers are one example. Around the time of Christ's birth, wealth was associated with righteousness and the priesthood was the source of authority. In some circles, that hasn't changed.

Too many people regard God as a transactional god. They say, "I pray this, so He has to do that. All the nice things I have done and what does it get me?"

Scandals have rocked Christ's church - on both sides of the Protestant-Catholic divide. Churches usually make the news only when there is something negative to say about them. In some cases, viewpoints of God are becoming more and more narrowed, to the point that I would not want that god, either, except that I know that is not what God is.

Another pitfall that has been around for ages are the people who think they have all the answers. They have God all figured out. And when they convince a cadre of followers, they preach sermons that scare the daylights out of the uninitiated and repel others who are just looking for something else. But it doesn't stop there. Word gets out and spreads like a cancer. You hear, "Don't bother with that Christianity thing; you come out either drained or depressed." Unfortunately, we all get thrown into the same mixing bowl, identified with the same stigma.

So, it regardless of what denomination you claim, there are those who will always associate you with a negative connotation they give to the name 'Christian.'

But let a crisis hit. Remember that old saying that there are no atheists in foxholes? Not far from the truth. When was church attendance at its highest in our lifetime and when did it start to decline? Check the records and you'll find that it started falling a few years after WWII was over. There was less strain over a real shooting war, the economy was great, everything was upbeat, and God was where? Did we misplace him? He's around here somewhere. Oh, well. Whatever.

French philosopher Simone Weil once said, "Humanity was not wrong in thinking that truth, beauty, liberty, and equality are of infinite value, but wrong in thinking that man could get these for himself without grace."

C.S. Lewis was once asked to point out the one big difference between Christianity on the one hand and all other major religions on the other and he gave a one-word answer: GRACE."

The world must acknowledge that God is the source of all grace. That is the starting point in turning around the decline in churches. And grace is such a multifaceted concept that understanding it is a journey in itself. Everything you hear in this church and every church stems from the light of grace.

We live in a world of no absolutes, only shades of grey. The light of Christ makes those shades clearer, sharper, more meaningful.

I once heard a story (which may or may not be true) of a cowboy whose hat was stepped on in the cow pen. It wasn't just crushed but was henceforth endowed with what we all know is found on the ground of a cow pen. He picked it up, slapped it across his leg a few times and placed it back on his head. By the end of the day, he barely noticed the bovine excrement and the random creases that made it fit funny. He felt no need to do anything different. Folks can get used to most anything.

Nonbelievers will make no progress if they do not first feel the need and see that this world, despite our attempts to adjust to it, is not the way God intended it to be. Even if you don't believe in God, do you really like things the way they are? Do you not see the need for something else?

Wake up! Smell the coffee!

We are the messengers of that need, that something else. Jesus said we will be known by our fruits. What fruits? Have you ever known someone who had a certain glow about their life, a spring in their step, a sense of outreach to those around them? Have you ever known someone who seemed glad to approach strangers and treated them simply as friends they have yet to meet? Someone who seems just glad to be alive and their joy, their simple joy, was contagious and you felt glad to have crossed paths with them, even for a moment? Their fruits, that's what you were seeing.

That should be us. From our fruits, let others wonder where our joy comes from. Let them ask. We'll tell them.

When their hearts are open, God steps in, and the light shines on a wonderful story of creation, love, redemption, and promises. God needs storytellers.

A flicker of light.

A promise of things to come.

Is that what I heard?

Questions for Discussion

1. Why is the Christian journey a matter of stepwise learning?
2. Is it possible that the more we learn and believe in God's love, the more human we become?
3. In the end, will those who are farther along in their journey have a greater reward than those just beginning?

Notes:

1. Philip Yancey, *Prayer,* (Grand Rapids, Zondervan, 2006)

Chapter Eleven
Debts? What Debts?

Romans 13:8-10

⁸Owe no one anything, except to love one another; for the one who loves another has fulfilled the law. ⁹The commandments, "You shall not commit adultery; You shall not murder; You shall not steal; You shall not covet"; and any other commandment, are summed up in this word, "Love your neighbor as yourself." ¹⁰Love does no wrong to a neighbor; therefore, love is the fulfilling of the law.

*****

When I was a young adult, the one of the most gratifying moments was when I paid off something, usually a car loan. When I finished my first tour in the Air Force, I wanted to go to my first civilian job debt-free. So, I dug into my savings and paid off my car note.

Silly boy.

Shortly thereafter, I needed what had been in my savings account, but it was empty. My first boss told me, "Never spend your own money! Spend someone else's!" He was a great advocate of using borrowed money and it must have worked, if you could see the house he lived in.

Not all debts are the same. Earlier verses speak of paying public debts. Paul advocated paying the taxes levied on the nation of Israel, even if there was great objection to them. There was ground tax which amounted to a percentage of what your ground produced, like grain, wine, and so forth. There was income tax, a portion of your earnings. A poll tax was included that was paid by everyone between ages of 14 and 65. Then there were other taxes such as road usage, bridge crossings, possessing an animal, scratching your ears, and so forth.

There have been those today who jokingly use one version of the Lord's Prayer as an excuse to say they owe nothing to anyone, and no one owes them. That is what it says, isn't it? Forgive us our debts...?

Sorry, that's not it. This chapter's scripture passage has to do with private debts, not bank debts. Christianity is not an excuse to overlook or refuse our obligation to our neighbors; that is, to love others as Jesus loved us.

When one does a favor for another, we hear the beneficiary say, "Thanks. I am indebted to you." Is that the debt of love Paul spoke of? No, but it's getting closer to the real thing. Jesus gave us that final commandment to love each other. In terms of debts, we owe each other our love. Is this a debt created through some transaction or something else? Why would Jesus care if we loved each other or not?

There are probably many answers to this question but the most obvious one to me is the fact that this world is broken, and it won't return to what God intended until we start loving each other and sharing the joy of the life God gives us. He made us to be relational creatures and we won't fit that template until we love each other as we love ourselves.

The subject of love is a motivator, a mystery, a misused and misunderstood word. Love has many forms in real life and there are examples of these different forms throughout the Bible. It is said that when Jesus asked Peter if he loved him, Peter answered in a form of love that was different from the form of the question Jesus asked. Most of us think of love in the romantic sense, as did Tina Turner. She said it was just a second-hand emotion. "Who needs a heart," she said, "When a heart can be broken?"

And yet, she was not that far off the mark. Some of the unhappiest people are those who are not loved, and not necessarily in the romantic sense.

The essence of Christianity on this earth is our relationship to each other. Jesus showed this when he met with his disciples on the last night and washed their feet. What did this signify in Jesus' time and culture?

Think of it: to love as Jesus loved. As he washed his followers' feet, toes, bunions, and all, he signified that it was okay to be human and to convey our own humanness to each other.

So, why should we care about others? Tell me, is it possible to be called a Christian and not be centered on Christ? Do you know of such people? If you do not center your life on him and the type of love he taught, you will be painfully unsuccessful in practicing your Christianity.

We all have a type of identity that we see in ourselves. It includes where we came from, what we do or did for a living, who our parents were, etc. Each morning when you rise, you unconsciously say to yourself, "This is who I am." The declaration is unique, very special for each one of us.

Part of that uniqueness is the Christian journey we are all on. Although we are looking at the same map, each one of us is at a different place along that road. The degree of dedication to the journey depends on your effort to engage God's help. Like it or not, your joy in any ministry will hinge on your dependence on God. It's like the giant beanstalk in which your dependence on God never stops growing.

How do members of our society view other humans? To avoid hours of debate, it's best to answer that question with other questions. Are we cautious? Trusting? Defensive? Gregarious? Something special? Apart from Jesus' commandment, how do we justify loving one another?

C.S. Lewis says the fact that all people are created in the image of God is reason enough to love them. Simple enough.

What human features do we share as we live in the image of God? Image of God – what does that mean to you? It's about people who have feelings, relatives, friends, a cup of coffee in the AM, likes & dislikes, a crush on a boyfriend or a girlfriend, things on their mind, many things that make them human – just like you.

The Hebrew word for mercy is *Chesed*. It has a guttural sound to it. It does not mean to simply sympathize with someone, but to really get inside the other person's skin, to feel what the other person feels, to see through the other's eyes. If we see our own faults in others, if we experience true *Chesed*, how can we not love?

If you read Mark 10:45, Jesus told us that "The Son of Man did not come to be served, but to serve."

Jesus knew who he was. And yet, he served. He came as a servant. If we know who we are in God, we will feel the freedom to serve and to care and to love and not worry about what it looks like. Why would someone not feel 'Freedom' to serve? Think about it. What would stop us? Do we feel someone else in need is undeserving? Are we embarrassed? Are we just unwilling?

So, how does love distinguish between servanthood and servitude?[1] Some people go through the motions of serving because of guilt, fear, or a half-hearted sense of obligation. Have you ever known someone like that? Have you ever seen someone try to love like that? Someone locked in servitude might be called a do-gooder or goody-two-shoes who acts simply out of a sense of obligation or perceived duty.

Servanthood comes from gladly doing in the name of God. It is with joy, purpose, and authority, doing the will of God.

Real servanthood flows from freedom; freedom to choose. Servitude comes from bondage to fear and guilt.

Servitude implies captivity, slavery, and involuntary labor.

Servanthood incorporates ideas of willingness, choice, and voluntary commitment. It incorporates a sense of moral indebtedness to each other.

Paul tells us that we should "Bear one another's burdens, and in this way, we fulfill the law of Christ." As Christians, we should seek the best ways in which to do this.

Burden is a tricky word. In a biblical sense there is a difference between a burden and a load. We see people carrying bags of groceries to their car. It is the result of the usual amount of shopping one does at regular intervals. These are loads one encounters in normal living. Each should carry his or her own load. A burden is something not part of everyday living, not part of an expected task, and something that Christians should take notice of when it encumbers others.

Distinctively Christian love is one vital aspect of evangelism. True Christian evangelism starts with caring. Why do we say that? Love is a vital motive for evangelism. It not another "notch" in the pistol handle. We don't keep score. That's not what it's about.

Good evangelism and good caring embody each other. The work of evangelism and caring cannot be done if we restrict ourselves to church walls. We must get into the world where people need the love of Christ. We must notice the needs of our neighbor.

Here's what Frederick Beuchner says about loving one's neighbor:

"When Jesus said to love your neighbor, a lawyer who was present asked him to clarify what he meant by *neighbor*. He wanted a legal definition he could refer to in case the question of loving one ever happened to come up. He presumably wanted something on the order of this: 'A neighbor (hereinafter referred to as the party of the first part) is to be construed as meaning a person of Jewish descent whose legal residence is within a radius of no more than three statute miles from one's own legal residence unless there is another person of Jewish descent (hereinafter to be referred to as the party of the second part) living closer to the party of the first part than one is oneself, in which case the party of the second part is to be construed as neighbor to the party of the first part and one is oneself relieved of all responsibility of any sort or kind whatsoever."[2]

Instead, Jesus told the story of the Good Samaritan (Luke 10:25-37), the point of which seems to be that your neighbor means anybody who needs you. The lawyer's response to that parable is left unrecorded.

You might ask, 'How much love is enough?' I realize that question does imply a certain intolerance and lack of patience. Nevertheless, if I am diligent and have demonstrated the love of God to another, and if, in spite of all that, the other will not receive the love of God, then I have done all I can.

The day-to-day steps of caring might not, on the surface, seem to be a witness to the love of God. It might not seem 'spiritual' enough. But meeting the needs of the whole person is always evangelistic. Do not limit God to only what you consider as "spiritual".

There is love and caring in the secular world because God is there, too.

Quality Christian caring is the embodiment of the gospel. As you do this, you are miniature Christs (in the words of C.S. Lewis) and you demonstrate the Christian message. Keep Christ's love in the background of your thoughts and it will show in your non-verbal communication, your body language, your face, your smiles, your tears, your laughter.

Hopefully, people will want to discover the source of the love you show when caring. They will want to find out what makes their Christian friends so special.

Frederick Buechner also said:

"The place God calls you to is the place where your deepest gladness meets the world's deepest hunger."[3] That 'place' puts you in direct line of sight of others who just may need your love and caring.

Ever wonder what God does in the heavens? Sometimes He seems so distant. I think one of His primary activities is listening out of love. He listens to us. He heard the Israelites groaning after He delivered them and He told Moses, "I have heard the grumbling of the Israelites." The psalmist writes, "God has surely listened and heard my voice in prayer." When Jesus stood before the grave of Lazarus, he said, "Father, I thank you that you have heard me. I knew that you always hear me, but I said this for the benefit of those standing here, that they may believe you sent me."

Through the prophet Isaiah, God said, "Before they call, I will answer; while they are speaking, I will hear."

Jesus said that greater love has no man than laying down his life for his friends. So true, but it is an exceptional example. On a more routine, day-to-day basis, the greatest gift we can give is that of ourselves, our time and attention. Love comes in many forms.

One of the best ways to love is to listen, really listen to others. This is not the type of listening in which someone is just using their ears, but with no intuition of the other's needs.

So, you can imagine that real listeners get involved. They empathize, they love.

As we read from the Book of James, we should be slow to speak and quick to listen.

To love by listening gives someone a sense of acceptance. People feel good about themselves when they know they are accepted. So much of our poor self-opinion comes from others who are poor listeners. And this is such a tragedy because good listening skills are something we can learn. Think of the tremendous effect on society if everyone could improve their listening skills by just 10%!!!

It's worth repeating: next to God's Grace, self-esteem is our dearest possession, our most treasured feeling. It is the center of joy in life. We're human! I either succeed in attaining self-esteem or forget about any future happiness. So, when you are a listener, remember it is not your self-esteem on the table, but someone else's. You can make a difference.

When you listen, I feel *understood, cared for.* I don't feel rejected. When you do not listen, or do it poorly, you say I am not worth the trouble!

So, we are here on this earth with an assignment, to love one another. It is an obligation, a debt God has given us, one we must gladly meet every day, and one we often fail to fulfill. At the beginning of this chapter, in the words from Paul's letter to the Romans, Paul tells us that if we love our neighbor, our subsequent actions have then met all the expectations of all the other commandments.

As we show our love through any method, we should make sure to affirm others. Recognize abilities and gifts in each other and take the time to mention them. Know that others are of equal importance to Christ as we are. Positive feedback always helps build up.

If everyone looked out for others, we would never have to worry about ourselves.

Nothing can motivate us more to look out for others than the realization that God looks out for us in forgiveness and grace.

Will it be work? Yes, and feeling God's hand at work in us as we love others gives us reason to feel blessed and joyful to be instruments of God's peace. And it will be the most blessed debt you will ever have.

Blessed debt it is,
Swimming in a sea of souls,
All in the same boat.

Questions for discussion

1. Why do you think God made us as relational creatures?
2. How is effective listening a form of debt payment?
3. For you, what is the hardest part about loving others as God loves us?

Notes:

1. The idea taken from Stephen Ministry training material, Module Four
2. Frederick Buechner, *Wishful Thinking,* (New York, HarperCollins, 1993)
3. *Ibid*

Chapter Twelve
Never-ending tale

Before I left Florida to come to Virginia, I spent ten very full months as interim pastor at my home church. This was a bit unorthodox, calling an individual to be a transitional pastor in his own church. Unorthodox because the transition period should be one of congregational reflection and evaluation of their direction and mission. The saying goes, "A new broom sweeps clean," and I was certainly not a new broom. But with the ingenuity of the mission committee, they did not need much of my guidance which made that part of my job easier. Nevertheless, I became a focal point in the church and, although I had known the weight of hard work in my previous years, this was different, and I was new at it.

There are several differences between my previous church and my current one, where I serve as Parish Assistant. But mostly, it's practically the same job in a different venue.

The point is, God leads us to various places with the same instructions to 'feed my sheep.' He never says, "Okay, that's enough. You can quit now."

John 1:1-4,14

1In the beginning was the Word, and the Word was with God, and the Word was God. 2He was in the beginning with God. 3All things came into being through him, and without him not one thing came into being. What has come into being 4in him was life, and the life was the light of all people.... 14And the Word became flesh and lived among us, and we have seen his glory, the glory as of a father's only son, full of grace and truth.

Matthew 28:16-20

16Now the eleven disciples went to Galilee, to the mountain to which Jesus had directed them. 17When they saw him, they worshiped him; but some doubted. 18And Jesus came and said to them, "All authority in heaven and on earth has been given to me. 19Go therefore and make disciples of all nations, baptizing them in the name of the Father and of the Son and of the Holy Spirit, 20and teaching them to obey everything that I have commanded you. And remember, I am with you always, to the end of the age."

* * * * *

These two readings can appear as bookends, with the life and ministry of Jesus sandwiched in between.

It is said that John 1:14 is the entire gospel in one verse. Look at it again.

I'm sure none of the disciples knew for sure what God was going to do. They did not pretend to know the details of God's plans. But they could see clearly what direction God was headed. They had spent a lifetime waiting to see the Messiah; a lifetime waiting for perfect peace. One thing was sure, none of them envisioned a closing chapter. The Kingdom of God is meant to continue from Jesus' time to our time and beyond. The last verses in Matthew's gospel clearly spell out what is to be done, but not exactly how to do it.

That is why a closing chapter in a book about the Son of God can be hard to write unless it is written with no ending expressed or implied.

I have heard it said that we are still in the midst of the creation story, that it is an ongoing work in progress, a never-ending tale.

The story line of humanity is a continuous story and God continues to reveal His purpose in small doses as He deems appropriate to our level of understanding.

And there is truth beyond that. For millions of people who have lived since then, the birth of Jesus made possible not just a new way of understanding life but a new way of living it. Like Paul Harvey, Jesus gave us the 'rest of the story.' God had decided the time was right and He came to us.

And Jesus tells us he will come again. There's no hidden message there. Plain and simple.

And so, we wait. There have been many who claim to know when the end of times will come and Christ will appear. I had someone ask me if this pandemic was an indication of the end of time. Jesus clearly tells us we will not know when that time is.

As the Book of James (5:7-8) tells us, we wait on the Lord Christ, like a farmer who plants and waits for the nourishing rains.

In the meantime, God, through the words of Jesus, has given us a holy template by which to live our lives. He has given us the pieces of the vision we can begin to put into place.

We, you and I, cannot have a vision of something unless our minds are searching for it. How hard are we looking?

Can we have faith in the promises of God in Christ? Can we speak the language of salvation, of redemption, of second coming, of living each day as though tomorrow would be the big day? Can we love God?

How do we love God? How does one show love to something or someone never seen, never touched?

We can learn to follow Christ by trying to live like him, letting the Holy Spirit guide us. We can learn from each other, support each other, admire each other, love each other.

We are told that He loves us and invites us to return that love. It's one thing to show what we believe. We do so by what we do in worship every Sunday. In our church sanctuaries, we have the opportunity to hear what we believe as well as to say, sing, and pray what we believe.

But wait. Anyone can do that. It takes no effort except driving one's car or walking to church, and God only knows if you really mean it once you get there. Going forward, let your actions speak for themselves.

Philip Yancey says, "The Master of the universe would become its victim, powerless before a squad of soldiers in a garden. God made Himself weak for one purpose: to let human beings choose freely for themselves what to do with Him."

Can we relate to that? Do we feel free to choose? Are we happy with our choices?

Know this: God works with a light touch, but he does work. So light is his touch, the side effect is that He gives us a sense of independence.

Such independence often feels like opportunity for disbelief. God's self-restraint gives an open door for those who would oppose Him. We would prefer that God overwhelm us with final proofs and certainty.

We want answers reduced to the lowest common denominator. We want to be justified by hard-core, reproducible facts that no one can debate.

On the contrary, Paul says we are justified by faith. That is, by faith we reveal who we are, who we are aligned with, in spite of the evil tragedies of this world, tragedies that try to challenge our faith and pull us away from the God who seems, at times, to do nothing.

In our faith, we recognize that there are others who live through tragedy and truly believe that God has forsaken them. Such events are opportunities to go back to the original question: How do we show love for someone who has been here and gone, someone we cannot see or touch?

In faith, we love what God loves.

We show the face of Christ to those who God loves because we are Christ's ambassadors to them. I do not think such a statement is in violation of Jesus telling us to focus away from ourselves. It is the obedience of Matthew 28:19 in which we are instructed to go out in Jesus' name. There is much to do, and we have all the tools we need.

> Tell me, show me, Lord,
> The question is where to start.
> Pray you will guide.

Questions for Discussion

1. Do you believe we are living in the *end times*?
2. What of God's work is yet to be done?
3. Is God waiting on us to make it happen?

www.ingramcontent.com/pod-product-compliance
Lightning Source LLC
Chambersburg PA
CBHW052141110526
44591CB00012B/1814